Creggan Community Restorative Justice:

An Evaluation and Suggested Way Forward

Marie Smyth, Jennifer Hamilton & Kirsten Thomson
Institute for Conflict Research
in association with
St Columb's Park House

ISBN 0-9541898-1-7

Table of Contents

	Page
Executive Summary	7
Introduction by Noel McCartney	9

Section 1 Background — 11
1.1 Background to Evaluation — 11
1.2 What is Restorative Justice? — 11
1.3 The Troubles in Northern Ireland — 13
    Post conflict transitions in communities
    Law and order and policing within communities
1.4 Restorative Justice in Northern Ireland — 23
1.5 CRJ in Derry — 24
1.6 The Creggan Community — 24
    1.6.1 Background
    1.6.2 Population structure
    1.6.3 Socio-economic status
    1.6.4 Social problems
    1.6.5 Alternative methods
1.7 CRJ scheme in Creggan — 29
    1.7.1 The complaints process

Section 2 Research Methods — 31
2.1 Research Brief — 31
2.2 The process and identified problems — 32
    2.2.1 Questionnaire design
2.3 The Research Operation — 34
    Focus group discussions
    Individual interviews
    Questionnaires

Section 3 Results — 35
3.1 Structure and operation of scheme — 35
    Premises
    Staffing of Premises
    Characteristics of target population
    Management of the scheme
    The identity of CRJ in Creggan

  Issues of sustainability
  Fire-fighting versus preventative work
  The remit of the scheme
  Future recruitment and protection of volunteers
  Extension of scheme into city centre
3.2 Young People's perspective   43
 3.2.1 Informal Contact   43
  Drugs and alcohol
  Perceived victimisation
  Links between the scheme and other facilities
  Facilities and boundaries
  Relationships with adults
  Interest in the community
  Gangs and locality
 3.2.2 Focus Group Discussions   47
  Perceptions within the community
  Young people's relationships with adults in the community
  CRJ as a policing structure
  Young people's relationships with CRJ volunteers
  Purpose of CRJ
  An alternative to beatings
  Improvements to the CRJ scheme
 3.2.3 Other young people's views   52
3.3 Volunteers' perspectives   56
 Low morale
 Overwork
 Recruitment of volunteers
 Support and ownership
 The nature of work
 Time commitment and hours of work
 Training and supervision
3.4 Local community leaders' perspectives   61
 Teachers' perspectives
 Individual interview with school principal
 Behaviour
 Paramilitary influence
 Relationship with CRJ scheme
 Dealing with authority
 Questionnaire

3.4.2 The priest's perspective	66
Problems and concerns with the scheme	
Violence in the community	
Perceptions	
Improvements required within the scheme	
Anti-social behaviour	
Local councillors' and community workers' perspectives	
Successes and failures of the scheme	
Improvements required within the scheme	
Perceived need for the scheme	
Remit of the scheme and training	
3.5 Victims' perspectives	72
3.5.1 Understanding the CRJ scheme	73
3.5.2 Approval of the CRJ scheme	74
3.5.3 Experience of the CRJ scheme	75
3.5.4 Feelings before/after the CRJ process	78
3.5.5 Improvements and changes of CRJ	82

Section 4
Conclusions, recommendations and ideas for the future   87

Feasibility of the model structure
Access to required resources
Geography of the CRJ Creggan
The process of building a support structure for the work
Principles

References   102

Appendices   103
    Community Restorative Justice Questionnaire   103
    Questionnaire: Creggann Report   106

Executive Summary

This evaluation of the CRJ Creggan Project commenced in February 2001 and was initiated by St Columb's Park House (SCPH). The Institute for Conflict Research (ICR) was approached by SCPH due to its track record in using participative action research (PAR) methods with young people. In PAR the community under study actively participate with the researcher throughout the research process from the design to the presentation of the findings.

The evaluation initially involved a number of scheduled meetings between ICR, SCPH and a group of young adolescent males to discuss the research and seek their participation. The young people were requested to assist in the design of a questionnaire to assess the views and opinions among other young people in the community of the CRJ scheme. The questionnaire was distributed to young people in a local school. A more in-depth questionnaire was provided to the teachers within the school to incorporate a broader range of views from local community-based leaders.

The group of young adolescent males also took part in a focus group discussion. CRJ volunteers also agreed to participate in a focus group discussion but requested that the discussion was not taped. Individual interviews were conducted with other local community-based leaders including a school headmaster, a priest and various politicians. SCPH also assisted by conducting individual interviews with victims who had sought CRJ's help.

The findings from the research are presented in sections, namely:

1. Structure and operation of scheme;
2. Young people's perspectives;
3. Volunteers' perspectives;
4. Local community leaders' perspectives;
5. Victims' perspectives.

The findings enabled ICR to suggest some recommendations and ideas for the future of the CRJ in Creggan. ICR recommended that CRJ Creggan required:

- Motivated volunteer committee members;
- Interested local agencies;
- Volunteer mediators;
- External expertise in CRJ;
- Volunteer support workers;
- Paid staff;
- Premises/offices;
- Drop in facilities;
- Expertise in supervision and support for workers and volunteers;
- Funding.

The availability of these resources will determine the feasibility of establishing a more effective CRJ scheme. In the course of our work, we have determined that some of these resources are readily available, whilst others remain to be secured.

Finally, ICR would like to thank all those who helped and contributed to this evaluation.

NOTE

Language in a divided society is often contested. ICR wish to point out that some of the terms used throughout this report, such as 'paramilitary' and 'Northern Ireland' are not universally acceptable. ICR has discussed the language used with the various colleagues involved in providing this report and has aimed to produce a report in language that is widely understood and acceptable. CRJ representatives discussed these issues with ICR and pointed out that although these terms are widely recognised and used they would prefer alternatives such as 'armed groups' and the 'North of Ireland'. For the purpose of this report 'Northern Ireland' has been used throughout and 'paramilitary' and 'armed group' are used interchangeably. We recognise that this is an imperfect compromise and hope that readers will accept the spirit of our efforts of sensitivity in language, even if some terms jar with them.

Introduction

I would like to take this opportunity to thank St. Columb's Park House for sponsoring this evaluation. I would also like to thank Dr Marie Smyth and the staff of the Institute for Conflict Research, Belfast, for carrying out their work in such a comprehensive and diligent fashion. I would also like to thank everyone who contributed to this report in any way. When St Columb's Park House initially approached CRJ (I) – North West Region we knew that a report on young people's attitudes to CRJ would pull no punches based on our knowledge that young people do not appreciate anyone who challenges their behaviour. However, we still felt that it was important that their views be heard.

On reading the report for the first time we felt that our fears were totally justified. However, after a more considered analysis we feel that this gives us a very balanced view of the project. We were delighted that only one of the adult interviews was critical and that overall the remarks were positive. We were happy that both political parties and the clergy saw the success and the necessity of the project.

We were pleasantly surprised that most of the criticism coming from the young people was based on perceptions and not on fact.

The concept and practice of restorative justice is growing widely throughout the world and, increasingly, it is being recognised as the future in efforts to tackle juvenile crime and low-level anti-community activity within local neighbourhoods.

Community Restorative Justice (Ireland) was formally constituted in May 2000; however the Organisation had been working in partnership with NIACRO since early 1997. In Derry, CRJ (Ireland) established a pilot project in the Brandywell area in February 1998 and, since then three new projects now come under the auspices of CRJ (I)- North West Region.

The legacy of thirty years of conflict has meant that there is effectively a policing vacuum in many nationalist areas of the city of Derry and that a violent informal system has been in existence for many years. However, in the context of a peace process, communities and agencies such as CRJ (I) have been trying to address these issues in a way that can change attitudes and point to non-violent ways of addressing the problem of anti-community activity. We acknowledge that this is an ambitious aim, but our experience to date has been extremely positive.

In order that we may increase the impact of CRJ (I) – North West Region, as well as improve the quality of service provided by the groups already in existence, we feel that it is vital to look to the longer-term and attract the resources necessary to sustain this project in the future. We feel that community restorative justice has a major part to play in addressing the issue of anti-community activity and improving community cohesion over the next number of years and we hope that we can build on the excellent work that has already been achieved to date by our voluntary workers.

We look forward to strengthening our relationships with other agencies, both statutory and voluntary, and continuing to increase our capacity to provide a service for the Creggan community.

Finally, and most importantly, I would like to thank all CRJ (I)- North West Region voluntary workers for their tireless efforts and commitment over the past couple of years in making Creggan a safer and a better community.

Noel McCartney
CRJ (I)- North West Co-ordinator

Section 1

1.1 Background to the Evaluation

This evaluation of the CRJ Creggan Project was initiated by St Columb's Park House in February 2001. Discussions led to the conclusion that some form of evaluation could contribute to the emergence of a clear view of how the scheme operates and how its operation could be consolidated and broadened. The Institute for Conflict Research (ICR) was approached to conduct this evaluation, which was funded in part by a grant obtained by St Columb's Park House from the Community Relations Council, and partly out of ICR's own resources.

1.2 What is Restorative Justice?

Restorative Justice, a method of addressing and resolving the problems caused by vandalism, theft and other forms of anti-social behaviour within communities, was developed in the United States, largely through the work of Mennonite Radical Reform tradition. Restorative Justice is based on a rediscovery and adaptation of traditional forms of justice found in Native American and Maori traditions (Wall, 1999). Its focus is on the disruption to relationships caused by anti-social behaviour, and the healing of those relationships, rather than any abstract of law, jurisprudence and punishment. The anti-social behaviour or offence is seen as disruptive to relationships within the community, and interventions are aimed at ending such disruptions and restoring goodwill in the affected relationships. Restitution rather than punishment is emphasised, and the participation of the victim and the offender is central to the restorative justice method.

In Table 1.1 the aims, principles and processes of CRJ are contrasted with the mainstream punitive or retributive approach that underpins the formal justice system.

(Source: Reflections on Restorative Justice in the Community NIACRO 1999)

Table 1.1

	Retributive justice	**Restorative justice**
Crime	Viewed through the optic of the conventional/formal justice system *crime* describes the violation of state order through law breaking.	For the practitioners of the restorative approach *crime* is viewed as a breach of interpersonal relationships.
Justice	In the formal/retributive view, *justice* strives to establish guilt for rule breaking.	In the restorative view *Justice* is conceived as the provision of a reconciliatory framework for identifying the needs of victims and the obligations of the offender/s involved in addressing those needs.
The Goal of Justice	In the retributive system the *goal of justice* aims to punish the law-breaker, in proportion to the crime and established guilt.	The restorative approach aims to heal or *restore* relationships, i.e. between offender & victim, and/or offender & community.
The Process of Justice	In the retributive system *the process of justice* is by design – adversarial, conducted by the legal proxies on behalf of the victim and offender.	In the restorative system *the process of justice* is based upon consensual dialogue, face to face, or with a mediator to provide opportunities for reparation, forgiveness and reconciliation.
Outcome of Justice	The retributive approach creates a punitive 'win-lose' situation that establishes guilt and dispenses punishment.	The *outcome of justice* is based upon the degree to which the needs identified by the restorative process are met and the obligations outlined are discharged.

In some locations, restorative justice has been used to address a wide range of offences, including offences against the person. Well-established schemes outside Northern Ireland address domestic violence and other serious crimes through the restorative justice method. However, within Northern Ireland, restorative justice has operated in a context where it is usually seen as a method appropriate to dispute resolution and relatively petty transgressions within communities. It has not been seen as appropriate for crimes such as sexual abuse, child abuse, or serious offences against the person, including domestic violence.

1.3 The Troubles in Northern Ireland

The purpose of this section is to a) explain the deficit in policing and the lack of consensual policing in certain communities in Northern Ireland; b) explain tensions within the Nationalist communities between Sinn Féin (SF) and Social Democratic Labour Party (SDLP) and c) outline the involvement of Sinn Fein in community policing.

Since 1969, and the outbreak of what has come to be called the Troubles in Northern Ireland, over 3,700 people have been killed in Northern Ireland, and over 40,000 injured in a conflict that has affected certain areas of Northern Ireland disproportionately.

The British government intervened in 1972, to suspend Stormont, repealed the power to govern Northern Ireland thus removing all substantial powers of local government, which were in the hands of local politicians. They also sent British troops to Northern Ireland in 1969. Initially the Catholic community welcomed the troops who they saw in the role of protector. However, the IRA was reorganising, and began a declared war on the British troops and the Royal Ulster Constabulary. (The British by then had abolished the Ulster Special Constabulary.) After the beginning of the IRA campaign, the British government instituted a policy of internment without trial, and prison camps were set up and filled with largely Catholic inmates. Perhaps of all British actions, the introduction of internment, together with the killing of 14 Catholics on a civil rights demonstration in Derry Londonderry in January 1972 (Bloody Sunday), consolidated support for the IRA in Catholic communities. Six of the fourteen killed on Bloody Sunday were from the Creggan estate. International attention was on Northern Ireland, and feeling in the Republic ran high after Bloody Sunday - the British Embassy in Dublin was burned down three days later. The IRA intensified their operations culminating in a devastating bomb attack in Belfast in July 1972 in which 8 people were killed.

The conflict has gone through many phases since the 1970's, but the death rate of the 1970's has thankfully never been reached again. In the 1980's the British government under a Labour administration redefined the conflict in Northern Ireland as a problem with criminal activity, not a political struggle. Roy Mason, Secretary of State for Northern Ireland, also instituted a policy of "Ulsterisation" whereby British troops were replaced by members of the (largely Protestant) Northern Ireland regiment of the British Army, the UDR/RIR. This was in response to the demands of a British electorate that was disconcerted at young English, Scottish and Welshmen getting killed in Northern Ireland. However, the increased deployment of local Protestants in the security forces active in Northern Ireland had the effect of further sectarianising the conflict, which was increasingly characterised by the battle between the (largely Protestant) security forces and the (largely Catholic) Republican armed groups.

Meanwhile, after the end of internment without trial, substantial numbers of people, the majority of whom were drawn from the Catholic community, were imprisoned under emergency laws and special courts. Initially, the political motivation of prisoners from armed groups was recognised in the jails. Prisoners were held in compounds and the command of their armed groups organisation was recognised by the authorities. The removal of the recognition of politically motivated offences met with strong resistance from both Loyalist and Republican paramilitaries, and some collaboration between them to resist this development. However, it was Republican prisoners who took on the British government – then under Conservative Margaret Thatcher - on the issue of the political status of prisoners. In the 1980's the protest escalated, and several no-wash and hunger strike protests culminated in a hunger strike to the death. The leader of the hunger strike, Bobby Sands stood in a by-election for the British parliament whilst on hunger strike and was elected as a Member at Westminster. On the second hunger strike led by Sands, Margaret Thatcher refused to concede and ten hunger strikers, including Sands, died. World media attention was relatively critical of the British government and quietly, in the aftermath, without apparently conceding anything, the prisoners' demands were met by the prison authorities.

Sands' victory in the election strengthened the argument within the Republican movement for ending their electoral absentionism, and members of Sinn Féin began to stand in opposition to the Social Democratic and Labour Party (constitutional Irish Nationalists) and get elected in Catholic constituencies. In the 1990's it emerged that the British government had maintained secret contact with the IRA from the early 1970's. Similarly, it emerged that the SDLP had been talking secretly to Sinn Féin and, in 1993, the current

Peace Process was launched which led to the loyalist and republican cease-fires of August 1994. These broke down, due to a lack of progress by the British government, who were depending on the Ulster Unionists' votes in Westminster for their survival as a government. However, after the Labour victory, the peace process had new life, although the traditional stand of the Unionists - not to engage in talks with Sinn Féin because of their links with armed groups - still caused continuing difficulty. However, eventually the Northern Ireland Assembly was established and ministers appointed to head the eleven ministries, including the contested appointment of Sinn Féin ministers to education and health.

To date, Sinn Féin's share of the Catholic vote has steadily risen. The Belfast Telegraph's Chris Thornton commented:

> Sinn Féin, however, is by no means finished. At the risk of creating a cringe-worthy campaign slogan, it appears to be the party of the future. Sinn Féin wins the young vote. More than a quarter of all 18 to 24 year olds (from a base including those who would not or might not vote) support Sinn Féin, double the figure for the SDLP. That translates into almost one in every three Sinn Féin supporters. Sinn Féin's age support profile – more than half its voters are under 35 – is exactly the opposite of the other main parties. These parties –especially the UUP with half its voters aged 50+ - had mostly middle aged or older supporters. (May 2001)

The current population of Northern Ireland is now 43% Catholic and 47% Protestant and Figure 1.1 shows trends in the comparative support for the SDLP and Sinn Féin.

Fig 1.1: Voting Comparisons - Sinn Fein/SDLP

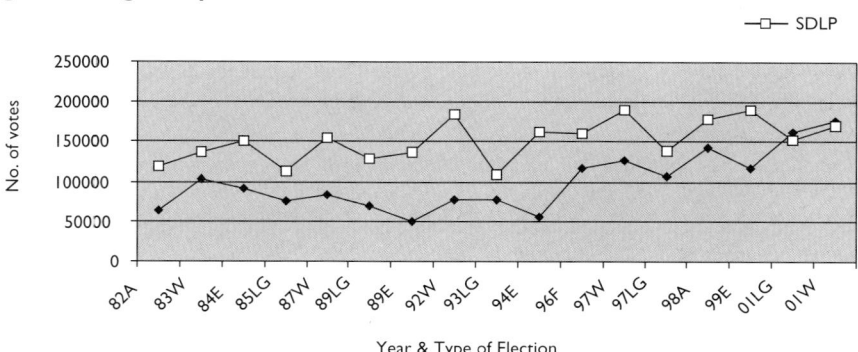

Year & Type of Election

15

Catholic and Protestant experience of the security forces has also been differentiated, with 4.1% of Protestant deaths as opposed to 20.5% of Catholic deaths being caused by the security forces and 0.7% of Protestant deaths compared with 2.8% of Catholic deaths due to the RUC. Attitudes to the security forces in general and to the RUC in particular have consolidated during the Troubles. In general the security forces have been regarded as largely unacceptable within the Catholic community. Following the ceasefires of 1994, the peace process and the establishment of the assembly a substantial demilitarisation within Northern Ireland has occurred and British troop numbers in Northern Ireland have drastically declined. This has led to the closure of army barracks, and the dismantling of some of the paraphernalia of militarism.

Generally, it was North and West Belfast and the border counties that were worst affected by deaths and injuries in the Troubles. However, many urban working class communities in Belfast and Derry were heavily militarised and paramilitarised.

The British Army, their local regiment - the Royal Irish Rangers - and the police (the Royal Ulster Constabulary) sustained heavy casualties during the Troubles, largely – though not exclusively, at the hands of Republican paramilitaries. Conversely, the fatal effects of the Troubles were disproportionately felt in the Catholic community. Over 43% of those who died in the Troubles were from the Catholic community (29.6% from the Protestant community, and 18.2% from outside Northern Ireland). Civilians account for 53.5% of all deaths (compared with 16.5% Non Northern Ireland Security Forces, 14.9% Northern Ireland security forces, 10% Republican paramilitaries, 3.2% Loyalist paramilitaries).

Post Conflict Transitions in Communities

In summary, the history of the Troubles created specific conditions within Nationalist and Unionist communities in Northern Ireland. Since the focus of this report is exclusively on a Nationalist community, only conditions within Nationalist communities are addressed within this report. Parallel conditions of alienation pertaining within Loyalist communities are beyond the remit of this study, although such alienation – albeit in a different form – exists. The Troubles has led to a situation in Nationalist communities such as Creggan, where militarisation, paramilitarisation and violence have been the norm for over 30 years. Furthermore, the substantial alienation between the local population in Catholic communities such as Creggan and the police force, resulted in there being no effective formal policing in such areas.

This lack of effective and acceptable policing coincided with the traditional alienation of communities, and young people within them from authority in general. Thus creating a culture of suspicion of authority. As the transition out of the Troubles began, concern grew within communities about levels of disorder and lawlessness. Local residents complained of high levels of vandalism, joy-riding, drug abuse, petty crime and anti-social behaviour. Outlets that were previously sanctioned by the community for adolescent frustration with authority, that were available during the Troubles, such as street fighting and rioting had all but disappeared. Increasingly disaffected young people began to be perceived as problems within their own communities. Reports of increased drug usage, increased levels of crime and anti-social behaviour led to a 'crisis' within many such communities. On the one hand, they did not wish to involve the police force (except in certain specified cases such as sexual abuse) and on the other they were unable to contain what they perceived level of internal disorder. In such cases, armed groups were often expected to intervene. These interventions began with warnings, and where these were not heeded, punishments became violent or offenders were asked to leave the country.

Contrary to the media images of them, the armed groups saw themselves as in the service of their communities. Thus, when the processes of demilitarisation following the ceasefires began, former armed groups – both those who were visible such as early released prisoners and ex-prisoners, and the less visible, those who had never been publicly identified – had to make a major shift in role. Prior to the peace process, members of armed groups used military thinking with all its associated characteristics. Military approaches to problem solving, and the kind of psychology that facilitates the use of force, may not transfer easily or unproblematically into 'civilian' life. In post ceasefires, new approaches had to be found; military thinking that included the legitimation of violent responses had to be set aside; and new peaceful (slower) methods and approaches needed to be developed. Those in armed groups and in the political parties that represent them retained the ethic of community service, and became increasingly involved in community activity and development. This was, for some, the continuation of a trend that had already begun earlier in the 1990s. In some cases this involved gingerly negotiating relationships with statutory agencies and authorities. For others, they could relate to the newly elected members of their own parties, who were now in local and regional government. For some, involvement in community issues and work was a challenge, involving 'a lot of talking' and frustrating those who were more action-oriented.

Republican former combatants had one important resource to fall back on. Their investment in politicisation of volunteers and political education generally within their organisation meant that most Republican former combatants had for the most part some idea of what kind of non-military service to their community might provide. Loyalist former combatants were part of a movement, which relied mainly on the ideology of defence (of the Union or of their community) and reaction to Republican violence and threat. They were – again for the most part - thrown back on Unionist ideology, which does not offer much by way of guidance in terms of community based politics. With the notable exception of innovative community development work in the Shankill and some other locations, the under-development of Protestant communities in relation to their Catholic counterparts has long been a concern of community development agencies. This underdevelopment has been documented and explored elsewhere.

Nonetheless, the transition was not easily embarked on in Republican areas either. Many Republican (and Loyalist) activists had spent all their lives including their formative years within an ideology that legitimates the use of violence in the pursuit of certain political aims. This inevitably increases tolerance for violence in general, and necessitates the development of certain forms of denial – the avoidance of full knowledge of the human consequences of violent behaviour. The shift to a position of adopting exclusively non-violent means to solve problems has been demanding of former combatants (Moholo, 2000: Knox and Quirk, 2000; Kizlos, 1998; Michie, 1997.) Furthermore, former combatants and others within political movements have had little experience over the years of being in power and authority. One Sinn Féin Councillor who took part in this research described how no-one in the Republican movement had much by way of useful or positive experience of negotiating or dealing with official authority. Such experience equips those in authority to exercise power with discretion, to adopt a measured approach, to avoid reactivity, to consider all forms of intervention including non-intervention or minimal intervention when managing difficult situations. For those who have no experience of the benign exercise of authority, this is a steep learning curve. For those without such experience and whose previous roles involved the use of lethal force, it is an almost overwhelming challenge.

It is even more perplexing in the context of a global society that has not yet produced effective and non-violent solutions to problems of community degeneration nor has it spent much effort on establishing expertise in how to repair damage to the social fabric of impoverished and divided communities. These problems are not unique to communities within a divided society. In the developed world, in countries that do not struggle with issues of nationality or the legitimacy of the state, the state of inner cities provide evidence that easy-fix solutions to these problems are not available.

So not only did these communities face the problems associated with the transition from violence to peace, with their capacity to change already compromised by poverty, deprivation and political marginalisation. These problems were compounded by the emergence, within that transition, of the problem of marginalised and disaffected youth. Some of these young people were so comprehensively disaffected that they evoked fear on the part of their own communities and families. This was compounded by a generalised societal fear of adolescent males, whereby the most innocent and law abiding youth can evoke suspicion by his mere presence.

The full emergence of this problem coincided with the emergence of the peace process, and the role shift of former combatants from their former military roles. This shift, combined with the ceasefires and the emergence of Republican and Loyalist constitutional politics, altered these young people's perceptions of the status quo within communities. Adolescent males, the developed world over, due to developmental and societal issues, related to adolescent rites of passage frequently identified with their local gang, gangsters, rebels or armed groups as champions of their anti-authority impulses. With the advent of the ceasefires, the admission of the political wings of paramilitary groups to constitutional government, and in the case of Republicans into ministerial roles, represented a betrayal of the anti-authority position that these armed groups represented for some young people. Yesterday's street-fighting guerrilla became a be-suited minister or local councillor or mayor, thus nullifying their value as role models for young people in marginalised communities with strong anti-authority impulses. If it is the experience of adolescents to oppose and challenge all authority, then when the anti-hero becomes the authority, their value as a role model or as a real implicit authority is lost.

Law and Order and Policing Within Communities

Some young people who took part in this study espoused a preference for the RUC. However, this was possibly due in part to their lack of direct experience of the police, since they do not patrol or police these communities where these young people spend a large part of their time. It was also possibly partly a gesture of defiance to the adults in the community who were adamantly anti-police. The anti-authority stance means that any potential authority will be preferred to the one that is actively seeking to exert control at that given moment. Since the Republican movement are the ones attempting to do so at this time, indicating a preference for the police is, in fact, an effective anti-authority gesture. However, this preference is composed of more than gestures of defiance. Young people have real and genuine grievances about the way the existing authorities exercise their power. Their complaints were of intimidation, of a lack of trust in the authorities commitment to non-violence, of unfair and uneven policing, of a lack of proper investigation and an assumption of guilt, and actual physical attacks in the form of painting, head-butting and threats of worse to come.

Figure 1.2 shows the trends in punishment beatings since 1988 in Northern Ireland, for all beatings and for beatings administered to those under the age of 20. A marked increase in all beatings is notable after the 1994 ceasefires, and a peak in the trend in 1996.

Fig 1.2: Paramilitary Assaults 1988-2000 All ages and Under 20

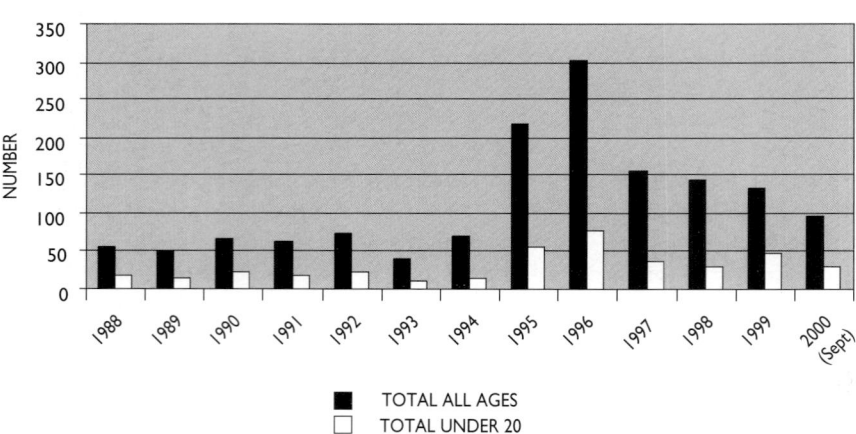

The IRA and other paramilitary ceasefires of 1994, together with the early release of political prisoners as part of the Belfast Agreement, and the population of such prisoners already returned to their own communities led to a re-evaluation of the role of former armed groups within their own communities. This re-evaluation led, amongst other things, to their increased involvement in a range of community activities. Members of local communities complained to these perceived authorities in their community about the anti-social behaviour that plagued them. As is apparent from Figure 1.2, initially, violent methods of punishing offenders were used.

Table 1.2 shows a breakdown of punishment beatings by Loyalists and Republicans from 1988 onwards. This shows that both Loyalist and Republican beatings tended to follow the same pattern, peaking in 1996. Some differences emerge after 1996, with an overall decline in the total numbers of Republican beatings, whereas the Loyalist beatings increased in 1998 and 1999. In terms of beatings administered to those under the age of 20, the overall decline in the number of beatings masks an increase in the number of under 20 year olds beaten in 1999.

Table 1.2: Casualties of Paramilitary Attacks: Assaults

Year	Loyalist All Ages	Loyalist Under 20	Republican All Ages	Republican Under 20	Total All Ages	Total Under 20
1988	21	8	35	9	56	17
1989	23	5	28	10	51	15
1990	21	2	47	19	68	21
1991	22	6	40	13	62	19
1992	36	8	38	15	74	23
1993	35	9	6	2	41	11
1994	38	7	32	7	70	14
1995	76	16	141	39	217	55
1996	130	25	172	51	302	76
1997	78	18	78	18	156	36
1998	89	15	55	14	144	29
1999	90	30	44	19	134	49
2000 SEPT	56	18	40	13	96	31

The picture for punishment shootings is shown in Table 1.3 and Figure 1.3. Since punishment beatings do not involve the use of firearms, they are less likely to be regarded as breaches of paramilitary cease-fires. However, incidents of punishment shootings have led various politicians to publicly question the status of various organisation's ceasefires, so shootings are arguable more politically hazardous to the political process, as well as damaging to their victims. Thus, there was a virtual cessation of punishment shootings in the period following the 1994 ceasefires.

Table 1.3: Casualties of Paramilitary Attacks: Shootings

Year	Loyalist All Ages	Loyalist Under 20	Republican All Ages	Republican Under 20	Total All Ages	Total Under 20
1988	34	5	32	14	66	19
1989	65	12	96	32	161	44
1990	60	13	46	18	106	31
1991	40	8	36	10	76	18
1992	72	11	61	20	133	31
1993	60	13	25	7	85	20
1994	68	13	54	15	122	28
1995	3				3	
1996	21	6	3		24	6
1997	46	10	26	7	72	17
1998	34	3	38	9	72	12
1999	47	12	26	6	73	18
2000 (SEPT)	65	8	36	8	101	16

Figure 1.3: Paramilitary Shootings 1988-2000

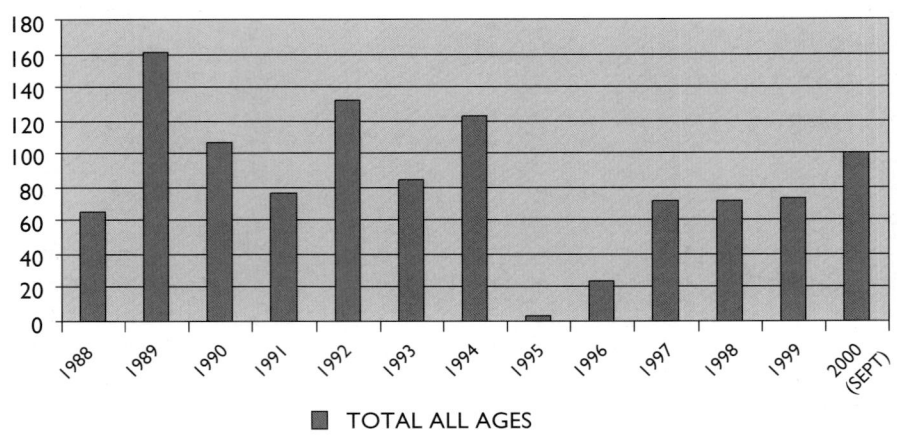

Some of the Loyalist shootings and beatings may well be related to the Loyalist feuds that proliferated sporadically during that period. Concern has been expressed politically that the continued use of violent methods by armed groups associated with some of the political parties involved in the Assembly indicates a less than total commitment to non-violence. The continued use of punishment shootings and beatings in the light of the rise of Sinn Féin into electoral politics has provided their opponents with evidence with which to challenge their commitment to constitutional politics and the legitimacy of their involvement in an Assembly where a pre-requisite of such involvement is a cessation of violence. The new political dispensation has led to the rise of a new breed of Sinn Féin politicians, councillors and MLAs with a youthful support base, and an interest in solving problems in local Catholic communities, such as anti-social behaviour and law and order issues. Yet problems of anti-social behaviour continue to dog the communities they represent, and some of their electorate consider violence to be a legitimate and effective method of solving such problems. As a result, Sinn Féin representatives report that they come under pressure from their constituents to promote and pursue violent methods of dealing with these issues.

1.4 Restorative Justice in Northern Ireland

Alternative justice systems tend to be stimulated and shaped by the social, political and socio-economic contexts within which they operate. In Northern Ireland, informal or alternative justice systems have evolved within both Loyalist and Republican communities, in response to the perceived lack of a legitimate or adequate police force, and to rising levels of petty crime. These informal systems, administered by armed groups, usually entailed an escalating scale of punitive sanctions, including threats, curfew, public humiliation, exile, punishment beating, 'knee-capping' and execution.

The expectations created by the peace process, and the new political dispensation, provided the impetus to replace these informal, punitive systems with the restorative approach. In the immediate years proceeding the first cease-fire, discussions were held both in Belfast and Derry among community activists, aimed at developing non-violent, community-based justice systems. In 1997, these discussions culminated in a document entitled, *Designing a System of Restorative Community Justice in Northern Ireland*, commonly known as "The Blue Book". The authors, Jim Auld, Brian Gormally, Kieran McEvoy and Michael Ritchie set out within the publication a template for CRJ that could be applicable within Northern Ireland. After consultation it was decided to create 4 pilot projects, 3 in Belfast and 1 in the Brandywell, Derry Londonderry.

In these early stages, NIACRO played a leading role in facilitating discussion and consultation around CRJ. In 1998, CRJ Ireland was established as an independent limited company with the role of promoting and developing CRJ within Northern Ireland and the Republic. CRJ Ireland currently supports 8 projects in Belfast, 4 in Derry Londonderry, 3 in Armagh, 2 in Tyrone, and 1 in Monaghan.

1.5 CRJ in Derry

Community Restorative Justice has developed an operation in the North West region, under the auspices of CRJ Ireland and organised by CRJ North West. Under this umbrella, schemes operate in Creggan, Brandywell, Ballymagroarty and Shantallow.

The Brandywell project in Derry Londonderry was established in 1999, following 6 months community consultation, and 6 months training of local volunteers. Interest in CRJ spread rapidly through the nationalist areas of the city. A consultative CRJ Forum was established to encourage inter-agency support, and to have a role in overseeing the development of projects. Representation on the forum initially included: local residents, NIACRO, clergy, Sinn Féin, and a lecturer (from further education). The unacceptability of the RUC in nationalist areas has meant that the RUC have no involvement in CRJ. There were no young people or youth organisations represented on the Forum.

The Forum now meets fortnightly and receives reports from the CRJ Co-ordinator, who is employed by CRJ Ireland. The Co-ordinator's role is to provide direct support and advice to the local projects in the Creggan, Brandywell, Ballymagroarty, and Shantallow. None of the projects have formal management committees. Training support for CRJ volunteers is provided by NIACRO, and covers: concepts of justice; values, guidelines for CRJ; legal aspects of CRJ work; human rights legislation; basic mediation skills; child protection; domestic violence awareness and an Open College accredited course on Restorative Justice. An outside body also provides stage 1 (3 credits) and stage 2 (3 credits) mediation skills.

1.6 The Creggan Community

1.6.1 Background

The Creggan Estate is situated on the Cityside of Derry Londonderry. The development of the estate commenced in 1947 and was completed in 1977. The 1991 Census indicated that 8,152 people lived in the Creggan. However, local community representatives and

Councillors have disputed this figure arguing the population size is closer to 11,000 (Meeting Local Needs, 1996). The estate comprises of approximately 2000 houses within the three wards, namely: Creggan Central; St. Peters; Creggan South and the 2 Enumeration Districts (EDs) in Beechwood.

1.6.2 Population Structure

Creggan, in the main, has a young and growing population. Table 1.4 shows the age structure of the population in the Creggan Wards, Derry Londonderry and Northern Ireland, highlighting how Creggan has a higher than average percentage of 0-14 and 15-25 year olds.

Table 1.4 Age structure in Creggan

Creggan Wards	% 0-4 years	% 0-14 years	% <25 years	% 25-64 years	% 65+ years
Creggan Central	9.7	32.8	49.9	41.4	8.7
St. Peters	12.6	32.6	53.6	42.7	3.7
Creggan South	11.7	33.4	50.2	41.2	8.6
Beechwood ED13024	6.8	26.7	46.6	41.8	11.6
Beechwood ED13025	4.3	23.8	42.3	42.8	14.9
Derry Londonderry	9.8	29.7	47.5	43.7	8.8
N Ireland	8.1	24.3	40.4	47.0	12.6

(Source 1991 Census)

The young and growing population has led to an increased demand in key service areas such as education, health, housing, pre-school child-care, recreation and leisure, training and employment.

1.6.3 Socio-economic Status

Poverty and long-term unemployment along with the impact of 30 years of Troubles have had a detrimental effect on the area.

Deprivation

Using the Townsend Index of Material Deprivation, which uses unemployment, home ownership, overcrowding and car ownership as measures, and based on 1991 Census data, Derry Londonderry ranks 25th in the 26 Northern Ireland local government districts with '1' being the most affluent and '26' the most deprived. Using the same index, the Creggan wards of St Peters, Creggan South and Creggan Central rank 4th, 5th and 6th most deprived out of 30 wards within Derry City Council area (Meeting Local Needs, 1996). Table 1.5 clearly reflects the level of deprivation in the Creggan community compared to Derry City and the rest of Northern Ireland.

Table 1.5 Townsend Indicators of Deprivation for Creggan

Ward	Population	Total Households	Not Owner Occupied	Over Crowded	No Car	Unemployed
St. Peters	2,141	571	85.6	16.5	75.6	41.1
Creggan South	2,353	673	83.7	15.7	75.2	41.3
Creggan Central	2,559	740	79.3	14.6	72.6	45.4
Beechwood	2,298	656	39.5	12.0	54.7	29.0
Derry City	95,371	28,026	49.4	9.7	45.4	23.7
N. Ireland			36.8	4.8	35.4	15.7

As Table 1.5 highlights owner occupation is only about 20% compared to Derry City, which is nearly 50% and the rest of Northern Ireland at over 60%. Unemployment figures are also much higher, nearly twice as high as Derry City and three times higher than the rest of Northern Ireland. Together, these figures highlight the level of deprivation within Creggan. For the next generation of young people these figures are not encouraging in promoting future prospects.

The Impact of the Troubles on Creggan

Derry City Council area ranks sixth out of 26 district councils in terms of their rate of residents' deaths in the Troubles (1.74 per thousand compared with 4.13 for Belfast, 2.48 for Armagh, 2.38 for Dungannon, 2.05 for Cookstown, and 1.89 for Strabane). Derry City ranks fifth in terms of deaths that occurred in the council area (2.50 per thousand, compared with 4.59 for Belfast, 3.93 for Newry and Mourne, 2.56 for Dungannon, 2.50 for Armagh).

Table 1.6: Troubles-related death rates and Robson deprivation scores for Derry wards

DERRY	Death rate	Robson Deprivation score
Altnagelvin	0.83	-21.99
Ballynashallog	0.71	-18.70
Banagher	0.83	6.77
**Beechwood	1.74	3.95
Brandywell	5.63	15.09
Carn Hill	0.00	6.54
Caw	1.20	-2.67
Claudy	3.90	7.19
Clondermot	4.42	-0.38
Corrody	0.85	7.81
**Creggan Central	1.43	12.70
**Creggan South	1.26	17.93
Crevagh & Springtown	1.32	4.69
Culmore	0.82	5.63
Ebrington	0.30	-3.07

Eglinton	2.07	-4.69
Enagh	0.71	1.43
Faughan	0.00	-3.36
Glen	1.22	3.81
Lisnagelvin	2.32	-7.98
New Buildings	1.52	-13.03
Pennyburn	2.34	-14.78
Rosemount	0.41	8.12
**St Peter's	3.80	14.74
Shantallow East	3.28	9.62
Shantallow West	0.49	12.22
Strand	2.61	6.76
The Diamond	4.95	9.91
Victoria	4.22	12.99
Westland	3.83	10.16
Average		
Northern Ireland	2.2	0

Source: Institute for Conflict Research

As can be seen in Table 1.6, the overall death rate for Northern Ireland is 2.2 per 1,000 population, and the corresponding Troubles-related death rates for the wards in Creggan are: Beechwood 1.74, Creggan South 1.26, Creggan Central 1.43, and St Peter's with the highest death rate, 3.8. St Peter's is the only ward in the Creggan district that has a death rate above the Northern Ireland average of 2.2 per 1,000. However, all four wards score high on the Robson index.

Education and Training

This lack of hope in obtaining full time employment has an impact on education and training. The 1991 Census figures for educational attainment, for those over sixteen years of age, reveal that 80% of males and 82% of females within Creggan left school with no educational qualifications. These figures are 20% above the Northern Ireland average. This suggests that the focus for young people must be on training to ensure that they acquire skills to improve their opportunities for employment.

1.6.4 Social Problems

Creggan in many ways is similar to other large urban housing estates, which experience high levels of unemployment and poverty, in that it suffers from the effects of drug abuse, alcohol abuse and 'anti-social' behaviour (Meeting Local Needs, 1996). However, these effects are compounded by the political situation and the cumulative effects of Troubles-related violence over the past 30 years. Policing has become a major issue within the community due to a lack of an acceptable police force among many residents. Thus, alternative methods of addressing these problems have been introduced.

1.6.5 Alternative Methods

Some of the alternative methods have taken the form of 'punishment beatings', mainly on young people, in an effort to curb 'anti-social' behaviour. However, punishment attacks are not viewed as acceptable by the majority and in June 2000 Community Restorative Justice (CRJ) was introduced as a non-violent method of dealing with anti-social behaviour in the Creggan Community.

1.7 CRJ Scheme in Creggan

During the early stages of the scheme an informal, ad hoc committee met to plan and co-ordinate its inception. It included representation from local clergy, school principals and councillors (SDLP and Sinn Féin). The committee no longer meets although, the intention is to reconstitute it formally in the near future.

The scheme is located in the Creggan Neighbourhood Centre at Central Drive. Initially, there were 15 local volunteers to staff the scheme, but at the time of this study there were only 9 active volunteer members. The volunteers are currently all male, aged between mid-twenties and mid-fifties.

1.7.1 The Complaints Process

Since its inception in June 2000, the CRJ scheme in Creggan has handled 118 cases. The majority of these cases have involved young people accused of petty crime, delinquency and general anti-social behaviour such as damaging property and creating noise. The scheme does not deal with serious offences eg. domestic violence or sexual abuse.

The volunteers receive complaints from those suffering from anti-social behaviour. On the main, these complaints are made by older members of the community about young people. The volunteers follow a procedure of establishing an agreed version of the facts (where there is no agreement then CRJ will not remain involved) and where appropriate approaching the individuals accused of carrying out the offence, or their parents, to explain that their behaviour is unacceptable. The CRJ aim to reach an acceptable solution and encourage a change in behaviour among the young people.

Section 2

Research Methods

2.1 Research Brief

The Institute for Conflict Research (ICR) was requested by St Columb's Park House (SCPH) to facilitate an evaluation of the Community Restorative Justice Scheme in the Creggan. ICR was approached due to its track record in using participative action research methods with young people. In PAR the community under study actively participate with the researcher throughout the research process from the design to the presentation of the findings.

As Community Restorative Justice is a community-based scheme, a participative approach in evaluating the output of the scheme was considered the best option. Since many of the CRJ's cases involve young people as either victims or offenders, the brief was to conduct an evaluation involving young people in the Creggan. The outcome of this evaluation was to be a report that could be used for funding purposes. It was agreed that ICR would work in partnership with SCPH and the Creggan CRJ volunteers in carrying out this work.

At the initial meeting with CRJ leaders and SCPH it was agreed that the work of the evaluation would be divided between SCPH, ICR and young people. This agreement outlined which stakeholder would be interviewed by which part of the research party.

The agreement was as follows:

Stakeholder	Interviewed by:
Project organisers	Young people
Perpetrators	Staff from SCPH
Victims	Staff from SCPH
Community representatives	Young people
Politicians	Young people
Other young people	Young people

ICR would assist in designing a brief questionnaire; prepare the young people to assist with the research and would analyse the raw data.

SCPH was responsible for securing the resources for ICR to carry out the work. All parties recognised that the available financial resources would not cover ICR costs. Therefore, much of the work has been carried out by ICR on a voluntary basis. This has placed a necessary limitation on the completion of the work.

2.2 The Process and Identified Problems

The evaluation initially involved a number of scheduled meetings between ICR, SCPH and a group of young adolescent males to discuss the research and seek their participation. These meetings were also necessary for ICR to establish relationships with the young people involved. The research team (ICR and SCPH) travelled on a weekly basis for ten weeks to the local centre where the young people gathered for youth club based activities. The meetings involved discussions around the following areas:

- The principle of PAR and what was involved so that the young people were very clear from the outset the purpose of the meetings;
- The role that the young people were willing to adopt in the research;
- Who the young people would be willing to talk to and who they wouldn't;
- The type of research methods that they would be willing to conduct;
- Incentives for conducting the research.

These discussions prompted reactions, which had to be resolved before the research could take place. It was clear that certain obstacles were inhibiting involvement with PAR and these issues had to be discussed with the young people to prepare them for the fieldwork stage.

Concerning who the young people would talk to, it was recognised that the young people had a 'comfort zone' in which certain groups and/or individuals did not feature. This 'comfort zone' was associated with the recognition by the young people that certain groups and/or individuals in the community would not be willing to talk to them because of how they were perceived. There was also an element of adolescent embarrassment about conducting this work in an area where they lived and concern at what their 'mates' would say. Acceptable compromises and solutions surrounding these issues had to be reached. These issues were further compounded by the fact that there was no adult representative to encourage and validate the role of the young people within the research process on a daily basis. The lack of daily support was due to no local representative within the community being appointed and ICR's geographical distance from the Creggan.

The research team recognised that for some aspects of the research it was not suitable to involve the young people. Therefore ICR and St Columbs Park House agreed to interview victims and (if desired) the local community leaders. Some young people expressed an interest in taking part in individual interviews, thus they were given the opportunity to assist in the interviews with community leaders. The research team suggested that the young people would research other young people to assess their views and opinions of the CRJ scheme. These suggestions were acceptable to all parties concerned, including the organisers of the scheme. The proposed method was also discussed and a questionnaire was considered to be the most appropriate method.

Through these sessions with the young people, the researchers also gained an insight into the CRJ scheme and how it is perceived among young males in the Creggan Community. It was also evident from these sessions that some of the young people had been through the CRJ process and could be termed as offenders.

2.2.1 Questionnaire Design

Having agreed the issues with the young people the research procedure commenced. The aim was for the young people to design a questionnaire to assess the opinions and views of the CRJ among other young people in the Creggan. These themes were identified as:

- Do you know what CRJ is?
- Do you think that it works?
- Do you agree with it?
- Are there any problems with it?
- Do you know how to make it better?
- Do you like it? Do you prefer it to punishment beatings/RUC/nothing?
- Would you rather stick with punishment beatings/nothing?
- How does CRJ make you feel?
- What do you get out of CRJ?

A questionnaire (See Appendix 1) was produced by ICR and distributed to the young people for discussion and comment. The suggested changes were subsequently made and a questionnaire with Yes/No responses designed. This format does have its limitations but was deemed to be the most suitable for the young people being surveyed.

2.3 The Research Operation

On completion of this session problems arose within the 'club', which were beyond the control of the research team. These problems prevented the young people from adopting an active research role in the wider community. The research team therefore adopted the following methods.

2.3.1 Focus Group Discussions

The group of young people involved in the design of the questionnaire were also willing to participate in a focus group discussion. The discussion focused upon their views and opinions of Community Restorative Justice in the Creggan, including its benefits and problems. The initial designed questionnaire (Appendix 2) was used to guide the discussions. Some of the discussions were taped and transcribed under the assurance that they could personally destroy the tapes after transcription. However, some refused to allow the discussions to be taped.

Focus group discussions were also conducted with the volunteers within the Community Restorative Scheme. The views from these people where essential as they are contributing a great deal of time and effort to the scheme. The volunteers refused to let the discussions be taped.

2.3.2 Individual Interviews

In addition to focus group discussions individual interviews were conducted with the local participants to assess their views and opinions of CRJ. These participants included a school headmaster, a Priest and politicians. Face to face interviews were conducted whenever possible although some telephone interviews were organised due to logistics. SCPH carried out the individual interviews with victims.

2.3.3 Questionnaire

The questionnaire was distributed to young people in the community through the local schools. A more in-depth questionnaire was provided to the teachers within the school to incorporate a broader range of views from local community-based leaders.

The findings from this research are documented in the next section of this report.

Section 3: Results

This section reports on the findings from the focus groups, individual interviews and other research activities. The interviews and focus groups were mainly conducted by ICR with the assistance of St Columb's Park House (SCPH) throughout the focus group discussions. SCPH conducted the interviews with victims. The findings are presented in several sections, namely:

- 3.1   Structure and Operation of scheme
- 3.2   Young peoples' perspectives
- 3.3   Volunteers' perspectives
- 3.4   Local community leaders' perspectives
- 3.5   Victims' perspectives

3.1 Structure and Operation of Scheme

Premises

When we first began working on the evaluation of the CRJ scheme in Creggan, we met staff in a community building referred to locally as *The Corned Beef Tin*. This building, which has a long history of community usage, is currently owned by the City Council. Creggan Neighbourhood Partnership rent the building and is currently negotiating a lease on it. The building had been closed at the point when local volunteers negotiated to have it re-opened and made available for use by the local community. The CRJ scheme is one of several schemes run in the building by Creggan Neighbourhood Partnership.

The building comprises of an office used by CRJ volunteers and other workers; toilets; a kitchen; a computer room used by evening classes; a hall containing two pool tables, some chairs, a table tennis table and a music system; and meeting rooms to the rear used by young women from the community. The location of the premises is central and accessible, but the researchers experienced some difficulty with the layout, since there was no private meeting space available in which to meet with groups of young people. Access the meeting rooms or the computer room is through the hall, so users of the main hall are constantly interrupted, making the hall only suitable for informal meetings and playing pool or table tennis. The office space was therefore used by the researchers for individual interviews and for meetings with the staff/volunteers. However, on occasions incoming phone calls, sometimes for CRJ volunteers and some calls about complaints about anti-social behaviour, made the office space unsuitable for meetings.

Staffing of Premises

The premises are staffed by a voluntary worker who is also a CRJ volunteer, who performs the role of doorkeeper, caretaker and supervisor. At the request of the researchers, another CRJ volunteer attended on nights when focus groups were running with the young people. However, the various roles and responsibilities of the CRJ volunteers and other staff in the building were by no means clear to the researchers, and this was borne out by a similar lack of clarity among the young people, who did not seem to be clear which adult volunteers were acting in which capacity. Adults supervised the drop-in facility, and CRJ volunteers came and went in the course of their work. However, some of the adults supervising were also CRJ volunteers. The dual roles of adults contributed to a lack of clarity about roles and functions of staff at any given moment. We concluded that the availability of more suitable premises, either by adapting existing premises and the clearer appreciation of adult volunteer roles would greatly assist the operation of the scheme.

Characteristics of target population

One of the striking features of the work of CRJ in Creggan, a feature that is also noted in some other schemes, is that the overwhelming majority of complaints are about adolescent males, although some complaints are received about adults and females. The main source of these complaints is from adults in the community. The main causes for complaint are petty crime, referred to as 'anti-social behaviour', and other activities such as alcohol and drug abuse, loitering, nuisance and making noise. Some of these complaints are seen both by CRJ volunteers and young people, as the product of adult intolerance or fear of young people. Whilst CRJ is inevitably driven by and reactive to the complaints it receives, some of those interviewed expressed concern about the concentration on offences or transgressions by young people. This could be a result of the way the community regards young people and their presence in the community, and the role attributed to CRJ. Some people were also concerned that CRJ does not deal with issues such as domestic violence, family disputes and other community order problems (CRJ refers such matters on to other agencies such as the Social Services). CRJ volunteers are merely responding to complaints - the nature and volume of these complaints is beyond CRJ's control. Some interviewees were concerned that, by expending most of their time and energy on complaints about young males, CRJ was reinforcing a negative perception of young people in the community. This negative perception casts young people - particularly young males - in the role of being the cause of the problems with law and order in the community. This was compounded, in the view of some, by the fact that all the CRJ volunteers were male. The gender composition of the team may lead to some people not using the team for such cases, thus limiting their usefulness.

Management of the scheme

In spite of various attempts to establish and maintain a local management structure involving key people in the community, there is no local committee for CRJ in Creggan. Volunteers meet once a week with a CRJ co-ordinator. Volunteers felt, therefore, that they were offered little by way of external support or supervision, and no formal community support in terms of a local management or support structure within the community. Volunteers complained about this, and expressed concern about the failure of the scheme to engage the active support and participation of the local community. This places enormous responsibility on the shoulders of a few people, and creates other problems, some of which are discussed below. This lack of participation meant that the scheme was associated in the eyes of the community with the small number of volunteers who operate it, thus compounding the difficulty about the identity of the scheme that was reported by the lead volunteer. Other volunteers also expressed frustration with the situation where local people complain about the scheme being identified with the Republican movement, yet those who complain are loathe to become involved and take responsibility for changing the identity of the scheme.

The Identity of CRJ in Creggan

In interviews it was repeatedly pointed out that CRJ in Creggan had the 'name' of being 'run by the IRA' or being a 'Sinn Féin-controlled' project. Whether or not this perception is accurate, it has the effect of limiting the sense of ownership by the community of the scheme, which is described by some of the young people as being the property of 'Sinn Féin' or 'an IRA front'. However, the only politician who ties in directly with CRJ is a SDLP councillor. This issue of the identity of CRJ arises in other communities, and in some cases may arise as a result of the involvement of some ex-prisoners as volunteers in some CRJ schemes. The researchers were surprised to discover that the young people used the terms 'Sinn Féin' and 'IRA' interchangeably, and made no clear distinction between them. The young people we interviewed told us that if they, the offenders, are visited in their own homes or taken aside for a 'talking to' by well-known ex-prisoners, political activists or those clearly identified with the Republican movement, they are terrified. This is because of the association of ex-prisoners and Sinn Féin with armed groups who have been involved in punishment beatings and shootings. The young people we interviewed universally regarded this as intimidating, and described how this situation gave rise to genuine fears and doubts that the non-violence pledge of CRJ would not be honoured. These fears and doubts had been recognised by Creggan CRJ volunteers who explained that some of the volunteers, who were most closely identified with the Republican movement, had decided to 'take a back seat' in an attempt to alleviate the problem of the identity of the CRJ scheme. However, this strategy does not seem to have been entirely successful, and the fears about the motivation and intentions of CRJ volunteers persist.

There is a paradox here. On the one hand, the young people interviewed who had had experience of the scheme as offenders complained that, in a tight-knit community such as Creggan, once a young person had the reputation for being a 'bad boy' that it was almost impossible to change that perception. The young people described how one of the attractions for them of the CRJ scheme was the opportunity it offered to redeem their reputation in the eyes of the community. Yet, on the other hand, some of the adult volunteers' associations haunt the young people or place them in a similar position, where their past reputation or current associations make it difficult for them and for some of those working with them to trust their commitment to non-violence. A great deal of frustration with this situation exists among young people and adult volunteers alike. The feeling of being stuck with a particular reputation, not being judged by your actions, but rather being pre-judged, was reported by CRJ volunteers and young male offenders alike.

In addressing these issues several factors will be important;

1. The avoidance of overloading any management committees or cohort of volunteers with people drawn from one political grouping, and the active inclusion of a broad range of views and groupings and both genders on such a committee;

2. An opening of dialogue in the community of their experience of violence in the past, and an acknowledgement of what that violence has done to them – both victims and those engaged in acts of violence;

3. Following from this exercise, the public reaffirmation of the non-violent principles of CRJ in Creggan;

4. A recognition in the community that healing relationships damaged in the past and establishing new and trusting relationships is the only positive way forward for Creggan, and that this will take time to achieve;

5. A commitment on the part of the entire community to grant permission to <u>all</u> members of the community to change, to develop new associations and aspects to their identities, and to develop new, positive and co-operative civic roles. The community must be encouraged to allow its members to be different in the future than they were in the past, and to support and encourage such change among community members irrespective of age, gender, past history or political view.

Issues of Sustainability

The issues of sustainability of the Creggan CRJ scheme seem to be linked with those of ownership of the scheme by the community. Unless the CRJ scheme can attract broad support from the community, a sense of ownership and participation, and an appreciation of its non-violent methods, it will be difficult to attract new volunteers of the right calibre and attitude. Furthermore, unless the CRJ non-violence pledge is understood and credited in the community, CRJ may increasingly find that an increasing proportion of their referrals may be from complainants who support a more violent 'method' of dealing with transgressors. This may increase the pressure and stress on CRJ volunteers who endeavour to deal in 'non-violent' ways. If CRJ fails to deliver such violent methods it's role may fail in the eyes of those who favour this approach. Simultaneously, if CRJ is perceived to be associated with violent methods, it may also lose favour with the rest of the community who oppose the use of violence.

Fire-fighting Versus Preventative Work

The current operation of CRJ in Creggan is focused on the provision of immediate mediation responses to complaints about anti-social behaviour, largely on the part of young people. The issues of the volume of work that the scheme handles in relation to young males, and the gender composition of the CRJ volunteer pool have already been addressed. The other issue that arises is in relation to the immediacy of the response, and the sense that the scheme is 'fire-fighting' all the time without having the time and resources to address more strategic issues. Preventive work, addressing the issue of who is setting the fires, and why, and how can they be prevented or deflected from doing so, also suffers under this way of operating. Volunteers expressed frustration about this, reporting that they were receiving the same complaints over and over again, and that the young people they were dealing with were re-offending. Some volunteers had concluded that CRJ didn't work, and even questioned the effectiveness of non-violent methods. These atittudes highlight the volunteers' disillusionment at the time of research but they were keen to point out that they had always supported non-violent methods and would still be volunteers in the CRJ. This raises serious issues for the design of the scheme in Creggan, and for its sustainability. In the view of the researchers, any future scheme must include the following elements alongside the mediation work:

- The inclusion of a preventive programme for young people at risk of getting into trouble; this could possibly be done in conjunction with the Creggan Health Initiative Project (CHIP).

- An intensive support programme for those who had already offended aimed at supporting the offender to adhere to their CRJ contract and to resolve any life or family issues they faced would improve the effectiveness of the scheme.

These additional elements would contribute to a reduction in recidivism and thus help to address the feelings of failure on the part of the current CRJ volunteers. This would be further assisted by the introduction of a systematic and reliable system for supporting, debriefing and supervising volunteer mediators and others working on the scheme.

The Remit of the Scheme

Those working in and using the scheme indicated fairly unanimously their acceptance that the CRJ approach was limited in its application to minor instances of anti-social behaviour. However, in schemes that run elsewhere, other kinds of problems are also addressed. In limiting the remit of the scheme in this way, participants are reinforcing the current dynamics and reputation of the scheme, some of which have also been regarded as problematic. If the scheme began to become more associated in the eyes of the community with mediating disputes with adults, or in dealing with offences committed by adults or against children and young people, it might be more successful in broadening the image it has in the eyes of the community. It is, therefore, important that the remit of the CRJ scheme and the kinds of issues that it aspires to address are kept under periodic review. Should the scheme become involved in a broader range of work, it would be important to ensure that a broad range of volunteer mediators were recruited, and perhaps some paid staff, including those trained and equipped to deal with children's rights. Such work would clearly require more intensive training and more in-depth induction into the work of other specialist agencies in the field, and how and when to refer on to those agencies.

Current CRJ volunteers described how they had been provided with training in order to fulfil their roles within CRJ. There was a certain amount of dissatisfaction regarding the expressed current level of training and a desire for further training was implied. However, it must be noted that CRJ Ireland has training programmes available that may or may not be availed of. It will be important to conduct a training needs analysis with the current volunteers, together with an evaluation of the previous training provision, so that future basic and continuing training can be designed to equip volunteers to deal with their specific roles within Creggan CRJ. The provision of training by other CRJ organisations within Northern Ireland may be problematic for reasons outlined elsewhere in this report, relating to the politics and geography of CRJ schemes in Northern Ireland. For this and other reasons, it would be advisable to tailor training provision specifically for the Creggan or the Derry CRJ schemes, and deliver such training within the community. In the future it may be easier for such schemes to participate in an island wide or European wide network of such schemes, but, for now, there are resource and other difficulties in achieving this.

Future Recruitment and Protection of Volunteers

As part of the visioning exercise for the future CRJ Creggan scheme, it will be important for scheme management to consider the breadth and size of volunteer base they wish to establish and maintain. Consideration needs to be given to the recruitment of suitable volunteers and the selection procedure for their recruitment. Scheme managers need to ensure that all new and existing volunteers are vetted, trained, supervised and appraised on an ongoing basis. This is in order to protect the scheme from liability in the event of a complaint against them or a volunteer. Such measures are also necessary in order to protect local residents from the infiltration of the scheme by unsuitable or dangerous people who wish to exploit the role of volunteer for the purposes of abuse or criminal activity.

All volunteers should also undergo basic training in child protection procedures and measures in order to ensure that they are able to protect themselves from spurious allegations of abuse, and know about procedures and regulations in relation to the care and protection of children and vulnerable people. All volunteers should also be informed about public liability issues and other relevant legal conditions and provisions.

Extension of Scheme into City Centre

The CRJ leader in Creggan described how he, the CRJ co-ordinator and several other volunteers also undertook to provide a mediation service in the city centre in response to the high level of violence at night when the pubs close, in addition to their work in Creggan. Undoubtedly, such a service is entirely desirable and necessary in order to prevent the kind of injury and damage to life and limb that currently occurs.

However, having noted the pressures already experienced by the CRJ leader and volunteers within Creggan, the additional pressures involved in monitoring the city centre presented a prospect of the complete overload of volunteers. Such overload is dangerous to both the health and well being of volunteers and to the standard of work that can be expected of them.

We would recommend that consideration of the provision of a service in the city centre by Creggan volunteers be regarded as a medium or long-term goal, with the immediate focus and priority being on the establishment of a solid base of support within the Creggan community. With this established, expansion of the scheme to the city centre or elsewhere can be countenanced. To undertake such expansion when the existing challenges within Creggan are unresolved would, in our view, be stretching human resources to breaking point, and is thus entirely inadvisable. The level of morale within volunteers, the level of trust among the wider community and the sense of ownership of CRJ within Creggan are all issues that endanger the ability of the scheme to survive successfully within Creggan. Therefore, these matters must be addressed as a first priority, before any consideration is given to the expansion of the scheme to the city centre or elsewhere.

3.2 Young People's Perspective

3.2.1 Informal Contact

The views reported in this section are based on a series of meetings with approximately ten young people who met with the research team each Wednesday evening over a period of ten weeks. However those in attendance varied from week to week with only three to four members attending on a regular basis. Although this level of change in the composition of the group posed difficulties for the research, it was significant that the same themes and issues emerged within each session. A further group of young people identified as 'offenders' were also interviewed in a group.

Drugs and Alcohol

During one session, one young man, under the influence of alcohol, attended a meeting with the researchers. The researchers observed that the routine use of (soft) drugs and alcohol was seen as 'normal' by the young people because the other young people regarded his behaviour as amusing and only slightly embarrassing. In this and in other sessions, discussion on drugs and the wish of the young people to see the use of cannabis legalised took place. The young people observed that adults in the community were habitually using cannabis but that use by young people was frowned upon. The use of drugs and alcohol in contemporary youth culture is not unique to the Creggan community, but is prevalent among young people. However, there is reason for particular concern about young people in Creggan, for a number of reasons.

Young people demonstrated knowledge of drugs and alcohol, if they knew or accepted the dangers involved in drug or alcohol use, this awareness served only to make drugs and alcohol more attractive. Therefore, lack of awareness or education about drugs or alcohol was not a central problem. Rather, drugs and alcohol were a feature of a battle between the young people and older people. Young people felt that they were 'punished' for drug and alcohol use, whilst such use was routine and heavy amongst adults in their community. Young people perceived this as hypocrisy, and this was a major grievance among the young people.

Perceived victimisation

This perception contributed to the young men's overall perception that they were victimised for their behaviour in the Creggan, whilst bad behaviour on the part of other people was virtually ignored. The young men pointed out that simply by standing at the corner shop, they attracted complaints, and this led to their perception of being victimised by the community. The young men's experience of feeling 'got at' is also reported by young men – and women elsewhere. Such experience on a continual basis can contribute enormously to the alienation of young people from the community, thus increasing their chances of participating in anti-social behaviour – since they get the blame whether they do or not, so they might as well do so. In the case of the young people interviewed, this feeling of being got at contributed to a situation where they felt victimised when they were barred from the club. Such comprehensive feelings of victimisation, in the absence of any positive or rewarding response to young people from the community makes it difficult for young people to see the difference between acceptable and unacceptable behaviour, since all their behaviour meets with censure. The existing efforts by CRJ volunteers to provide positive rewards for the young men are to be commended, but require to be built upon, and other agencies in the community must be persuaded to positively re-orient themselves towards the community's young people, particularly its young men.

Links Between the Scheme and Other Facilities

The drop-in club in which the researchers met the young people was separate from the CRJ scheme, yet had close links with it. Many of the youth leaders in the drop-in were also CRJ volunteers. The nature of the links between the two organisations, and the 'hats' that youth leaders or CRJ volunteers were wearing at any one time was a source of confusion for the young people (and indeed the research team, as outsiders to the community!) The young people also professed confusion about purpose and structure of the CRJ. However, this reported confusion dissipated during the focus group discussions, where the young people displayed a detailed knowledge of the operations, personnel and structures of CRJ.

Facilities and Boundaries

The young people said that, in spite of having access to the youth club, they were restricted in terms of when they could come and go and what they could do. They indicated that they needed a place to go 24 hours a day and 7 days a week. There may be difficulties about the feasibility of such provision, but the expressed need on the part of the young people reinforces the sense that there was 'no space' for them in the community, and that when they were out on the streets, they attracted complaints and criticism. The young people said that they would prefer to have more input to the running of such a provision than they currently have. However, to achieve this, more trust would have to be built between the young people and the adults of the community.

The young people saw the current restrictions placed on them by adult leaders as not being clear or consistent. During one session with the researchers, the setting of boundaries and formalising rules and limits of behaviour were discussed. This arose from a specific incident, which had occurred in the club the previous night, where a violent incident had allegedly taken place. The young people suggested that some clear set of regulations were necessary. They enthusiastically formulated a list of rules for the club (leaders and young people) and with some encouragement listed rules more specifically for the young people. The list of rules included:

- No violence in the club;
- No alcohol in the club;
- No-one under the influence of alcohol in the club;
- Smoking in the 'smoke room' only;
- Consideration of others when turning up the radio volume;
- No weapons allowed, and no use of club equipment (such as pool cues) as weapons;
- No drugs in the club;
- Respect club equipment and property (e.g. no standing on pool tables);
- No under 14's allowed in the club.

However, the young people found formulating appropriate 'consequences' for when rules are broken more difficult, especially if they thought they themselves were the guilty party. Their difficulty in formulating punishments was due to their inability to identify levels of 'punishment' that fitted the 'crime'. Some of the young people did recognise that different levels of punishment were required, so that punishment could be increased or decreased. In discussion, for example, they suggested that if the 'No violence rule was broken' the punishment would depend on the type of violence. Physical violence would result in being barred from the club ('Out') but they were unable to identify levels of physical violence, or different scales of punishment. Exclusion seemed to be the only method of punishment they could identify. When the researchers asked about suitable punishments for various levels of violence the young people, thought that verbal violence should merit being banned for a period of time, but if the offence was repeated three times the offender would be 'Out' indefinitely.

This led to the conclusion that an agreed and more sophisticated and graded system of 'consequences' that could be consistently applied to various levels of offending behaviour would improve the functioning of the scheme. Such a system would need to be fair, transparent, and the 'punishment' should be seen to fit the 'crime'. Futhermore, in order to satisfy the young people's expressed desire for redemption of their reputations in the eyes of the community, the application of 'punishments' that are of use and service to the community (whilst avoiding public humiliation) might be worth developing.

Relationships with Adults

The young people admitted that at times they did behave in a manner, which provoked adult anger, and as a result, relationships with the adults of the community were notably strained. However, it was clear that the young people desired positive adult attention and affirmative interaction with adults, yet a lack of mutual trust prevented this from occurring. The group named specific adults from whom they did receive such attention, but it was apparent to the young people that these adults were near 'burnout' stage due to their level of commitment to the CRJ scheme. One adult in particular had gained great respect and trust among the young people. However, the young people recognised the immense burden that one individual carried, and expressed their concern for his continued ability to perform this role.

Interest in the Community

The apparent lack of positive adult interaction contributed to the young people's alienation from their community. There was a sense that the young people could only see the negative aspects of the community creating a sense of 'hopelessness' among them. This hopelessness, as well as being a product of their alienation, also reinforced it. During one session the researcher asked the young people to focus on the positive aspects of the community, and many of the young men found this difficult, if not impossible.

Gangs and Locality

Throughout the course of the discussions it became apparent that the young people in the area form various neighbourhood gangs and only certain gangs use certain facilities in the area. Each gang has its own territory and Creggan is clearly divided into two territories, Upper and Lower Creggan. The club is situated in Upper Creggan and the gangs in this area do not welcome gangs from the lower area entering their domain. Conversely, the youth club is situated in Lower Creggan. Thus, for young people in the

Creggan, conflict is not only experienced between themselves and adults, conflict is also manifest amongst young people themselves. This fragmentation amongst young people creates a further challenge to service providers in the area, and to those who would seek to involve young people in community affairs.

3.2.2 Focus Group Discussions

The young people were also divided into three focus groups and interviewed according to an interview schedule that they helped to design (see Appendix 2). A number of issues emerged:

- Perceptions within the community
- Young people's relationship with adults in the community
- CRJ as a policing structure
- Young people's relationship with CRJ volunteers
- Purpose of CRJ

Perceptions Within the Community

Creggan is a tight knit community and consequently reputations of individuals and/or groups within the community can be difficult to change once established. These reputations may be linked with the family's history or a specific notorious action of an individual family member. In the view of the young people interviewed, adults' perceptions in the community associate them – the young people – with problems of noise, theft, and other nuisance or threat to the community's well being. The young people acknowledged that in certain situations the complaints being made were justified. On other numerous occasions, however, complaints were unfounded or unjustified in their view. They felt that by *"just by having a pulse"* a young person got into trouble, or *"just being seen"* with a group was sufficient stimulus for complaints to be directed at them. Some young people reported that once labelled within the community as a 'troublemaker', the reputation and label remained fixed: *"once a hood, always a hood"*. One young person reported, *"if you get a bad name in the community, you will get blame all the time. You will get blamed for stealing everything ... then they find out later that it was not us or it was him"*. As a result, the young people felt hopeless about the prospect of positive change - things were *"never going to change - so what is the point of all of this [research]?"* Some of the young people thought that they just had to accept the situation as it was, and that this stigmatised and marginalised position within the community was simply their lot in life.

Young Peoples' Relationship with Adults in the Community

In interview, the young people reported alienation between themselves and adult members of the community. This was marked by a comprehensive lack of trust of others. Some young people expressed the attitude that *"they could only trust their close family and friends"* and others stated that they were not able to trust anyone else in the community.

The young people explained the dynamic set up between themselves and adults. Adults perceive young people as the 'problem': young people, in turn, perceive adults as being 'complainers'. The young people saw some of the adult complaints as a product of adults' lives in the community. They explained some of the adults' complaints as unjustified, a result of adults having nothing better to do than complain – *"the complainers... they have no lives! They have no lives! That is what is wrong with them!"*

Some of the young people related this to what they perceived as the hypocrisy of adults in the community. The young people felt that although adults could acceptably consume alcohol and drugs, these same adults expressed disapproval at young people for following their example. Some young people thought that the adults who were most at fault in this way were *"the ones that are doing the complaining, they are the ones that are doing things as well"*. Some of the young people felt a strong sense of injustice as a result, that they were punished and castigated for behaviour that was prevalent in the community. Accompanying this, young people expressed a strong desire to be able to make choices about their own lives.

CRJ as a Policing Structure

Young people compared the CRJ scheme to their own experiences of paramilitary and RUC policing methods. They did not see the CRJ scheme as a real alternative to other forms of punishment. The young people emphasised their view of CRJ as retributive, and their distrust of the comprehensiveness of CRJ's commitment to non-violent methods. They perceived the non-violent methods used by CRJ as merely the first in a range of disposals that might be used against them in the long run. Of the CRJ non-violent methods of intervention, one young person said, *"if you do it again, they come back, they come [back] with some guns"*. The young people's accounts of adults dealing with their offending behaviour depicted the use of violent methods if non-violent methods were seen as ineffective, *"and if they don't get sorted out, they just batter us"*. It must be clearly stated that the young people were not alleging that the CRJ volunteers we interviewed were involved in violence against them, but rather that the young people saw them as [the more acceptable and non-violent] part of an adult system that also used violence and humiliation as methods of punishing young people.

Some young people interviewed saw similarities between the police and CRJ procedures in investigating a complaint. In both cases, this procedure involved coming to the house, talking to the parents and the offender and administering some sort of punishment. For other young people, CRJ was seen as an alternative, but only in certain circumstances. Within the focus group discussions, young people recognised the *"need for a neutral force"*. They thought that this *"neutral force"* or group would not be associated with the RUC or paramilitaries, yet should be able to deal with the difficulties within the community.

Young People's Relationships with CRJ Volunteers

Young people interviewed pointed out that only a small number of the adults were actively working in the community. Therefore, it was inevitable that these adults had to carry out a number of different tasks and assume many different roles. However, young people reported concern about what they perceived to be an insufficiently clear demarcation between the political (or alleged paramilitary) roles of a number of the adults involved in the CRJ scheme. There was a lack of trust about non-violent methods being used. The young people said that they did not respect the IRA because *"they sell drugs"* and *"they give beatings"*. Therefore, their attitude and relationship toward those CRJ volunteers they perceived to be linked with the IRA was negative:

"They think they're superior – I don't respect them, don't look up to them in any way. You are arrogant and untouchable if you are in the IRA".

Young people expressed confusion and a lack of trust about who actually managed the scheme. Thus, whatever the reality, CRJ was perceived by the young people to be run by specific interest groups within the community, rather than being accountable to the entire community.

It is perhaps inevitable in a tight knit community that the young people held different attitudes to various CRJ volunteers. CRJ volunteers are members of the same community so they often have a history and a 'name' within the community. This knowledge of the various volunteers impacted on the young person's attitudes and assessment of the effectiveness and trustworthiness of the CRJ scheme. There was, however, recognition and admiration for some of the volunteers working within the scheme – *"Well, there is one good boy in it and that is the only boy that I would talk to and trust"*. The young people also realised that the CRJ personnel were volunteers and it was thought that *"some were all right, some have a good heart"*. However, other comments indicated a resistance to CRJ intervention. The association between the Republican movement and some of the CRJ volunteers discussed above was a factor in these perceptions.

The effectiveness of the CRJ intervention also seemed to be associated with the specific personalities of volunteers, according to the young people. Success and the outcome of the mediation depended on the person that arrives to mediate. Young people's experience of mediation, not surprisingly, affected the way in which they perceived the effectiveness of the scheme. One young man told researchers: *"it works good enough ... it all depends on who or what member it is that comes around"*. Others were less positive, again, possibly because of the lack of trust and respect noted above. For some young people the scheme was perceived as *"interfering with peoples business"*. Some other young people complained that facts around specific allegations had not been properly ascertained and judgements and adjudications were made in situations where *"they* [CRJ volunteers] *jump to conclusions"*. However, as was highlighted earlier CRJ do not conduct investigations but merely report allegations to parents.

Purpose of CRJ

Most young people had an understanding of the purpose of the CRJ scheme in Creggan, *"CRJ try and sort it out, they talk about conflict"*. The scheme makes use of non-violence; voluntary participation from community members; and meetings and discussions between victims and the offenders about the offence and the consequence of the offending behaviour. There was an agreement among the young people that the CRJ process attempts to give the offender an opportunity to think about what they have done and to arrive at an appropriate response to the behaviour. *"CRJ makes you think about what you have done"*. For some of the young people, CRJ was seen as a *"second chance"* that offered the potential for them to redeem their good name in the community. One young man told us that CRJ *"may change your name in the community"*. The difficulty in 'changing ones name' in a community as tight-knit as Creggan was noted. Nonetheless, young people thought that CRJ could help realise this goal, through trying to *"give you some good and all, like if you are doing stuff for the community and giving back to the community ... community work and all"*.

Young people told us that CRJ intervention was effective with young people whose parents take it seriously, but *"some kids are at the stage where they don't care what their Ma says"*.

An Alternative to Beatings

Young people saw the scheme as having the potential to be an alternative to beatings. They reported a fear of being attacked or beaten and felt that being part of the CRJ scheme could help one *"avoid an early death"* or participation in CRJ *"may stop you from being beaten"*. Some young people held the view that *"beatings do not change a person, but make them worse"*. One young person told us that punishment beatings were a bad idea because of the dynamic they set up within the community:

"…people rebel more against the people who are giving them out. It's intimidation, and you want to defy them … Where do they get their authority? … If you have a gun … if they have no guns they have no authority …".

This creates a dangerous dynamic within communities, with some young people expressing a preference for *"taking your beating and getting on with it"* rather than colluding with what they see as the hypocrisy of adults. However, some young people expressed scepticism and ambivalence about the scheme because of the way that they had seen cases handled and the way that they had observed the scheme operating within the community. Whilst some of this scepticism is undoubtedly related to the shortcomings of the scheme, some of it might also be related to adolescent desire to behave in an unbridled manner with impunity. In the round, however, the researchers formed the impression that if any form of control over behaviour was required, (and some of the young informants would hold the view that none was), then CRJ was the best of the available options, even though it could be substantially improved.

Improvements to the CRJ Scheme

When exploring the improvements of the scheme with the young people, young people suggested that a younger group of volunteers be recruited in order to better relate to the young people in the community. The volunteers were described as *"not people our age ... about late 20's or 30's – but they would understand us better than people that are 50 odd"*. Elsewhere, some volunteers were referred to as *"past his sell-by date"*.

A change of personnel in the CRJ scheme management was suggested by the young people, in order to improve the scheme's effectiveness. One young man reported that the scheme was *"not run properly and they need community workers"*. Young people thought it would be beneficial if 'outsiders' could participate in running the scheme, in order to counterbalance the negative and entrenched perceptions within the community. Such outsiders were seen as less biased: *"They won't know the 'names' they will be fresh"*. Outsiders could focus on the facts of the complaint and not getting caught up in the community prejudices. They *"would be able to work with us better... won't have any hang ups or judge us on our background"*. For the young people interviewed, prior knowledge within the community is not always compatible with justice and due process, and reputations within the community play an important part in attributing 'blame' for offences committed.

3.2.3 Other Young People's Views

The questionnaire designed by the initial group of young people was distributed to pupils in two classes at St. Peter's High school (Appendix 1). Sixty questionnaires were completed by males aged between 12 and 17 years of age. The questionnaire aimed to ascertain the attitudes and views of the Creggan CRJ scheme among the wider peer group of other young people, some of whom were not directly involved in CRJ.

St Peter's is an all male school serving the Creggan community, with a reputation for containing many of the young men who are potential or actual CRJ customers. Of the young people surveyed 31.7% admitted to having direct experience of the CRJ scheme although the nature of their experience was not elicited. Table 3.1 shows the age breakdown of respondents.

Table 3.1

Age

		Frequency	Percent	Valid Percent	Cumulative Percent
Valid	12-14 years	35	58.3	58.3	58.3
	15-17 years	25	41.7	41.7	100.0
	Total	60	100.0	100.0	

Table 3.2 shows that almost half of the boys, 46.7% of the sample, knew what CRJ was. The following responses are based on the 46.7% who knew what CRJ was. A quarter, 25.0%, felt that it was a good alternative to a police force (Table 3.3). This would confirm the interview data on attitudes to CRJ.

Table 3.2

Do you know what CRJ is?

		Frequency	Percent	Valid Percent	Cumulative Percent
Valid	yes	28	46.7	46.7	46.7
	no	32	53.3	53.3	100.0
	Total	60	100.0	100.0	

Table 3.3

Do you think it is a good alternative?

		Frequency	Percent	Valid Percent	Cumulative Percent
Valid	yes	7	25.0	25.9	25.9
	no	20	71.4	74.1	100.0
	Total	27	96.4	100.0	
Missing	System	1	3.6		
Total		28	100.0		

Nearly two thirds, 64.3%, of the young people, who were familiar with what CRJ was, identified it as being a non-violent approach to deal with problems in the community. However, 35.7%, thought that it was not non-violent, again confirming the scepticism found in the interviews with young people. When asked if the CRJ scheme worked well, respondents' opinions were almost equally divided, with 46.4% saying yes and 50.0% saying no. However, 85.7% were of the opinion that it had some effect on crime levels (see Table 3.4).

Table 3.4

Do you think that CRJ affects crime?

		Frequency	Percent	Valid Percent	Cumulative Percent
Valid	yes	24	85.7	85.7	85.7
	no	4	14.3	14.3	100.0
	Total	28	100.0	100.0	

Responses to further questions indicated that respondents saw the effectiveness of CRJ as related to the severity of the crime, with CRJ being more effective for minor crimes than for serious crimes (Tables 3.5 and 3.6).

Table 3.5

Do you think it works for serious crime?

		Frequency	Percent	Valid Percent	Cumulative Percent
Valid	yes	11	39.3	39.3	39.3
	no	17	60.7	60.7	100.0
	Total	28	100.0	100.0	

Again, this reflects the views found amongst young people and volunteers alike about the limitations of the usefulness of CRJ in cases of serious crime.

Table 3.6

Do you think it works for minor crime?

		Frequency	Percent	Valid Percent	Cumulative Percent
Valid	yes	17	60.7	60.7	60.7
	no	11	39.3	39.3	100.0
	Total	28	100.0	100.0	

In spite of these limitations 64.3% of the young people felt that CRJ was a good idea. However, opinions were divided about how it is run in the Creggan with 39.3% agreeing with how it was currently run compared to 53.6% who disagreed (see Table 3.7). This division of views was also found in the focus group discussions, which also shed light on the rationale behind this view, and why young people feel the way they do.

Table 3.7 **Do you agree with how it is run in the Creggan?**

		Frequency	Percent	Valid Percent	Cumulative Percent
Valid	yes	11	39.3	42.3	42.3
	no	15	53.6	57.7	100.0
	Total	26	92.9	100.0	
Missing	System	2	7.1		
Total		28	100.0		

When asked about the volunteers of the scheme 71.4% felt that the workers were good at sorting out problems in a non-violent way but 85.7% would still like to see the scheme being improved. The questionnaire did not permit further exploration of this issue but the focus group discussions provided an insight into how some of the young people would like to see the scheme improved. The questionnaire did, however, reveal that 82.1% of the young people feel that the scheme requires more money so that it can operate better.

Opinions of the system for dealing with complaints were also divided. The system was acceptable to 53.6% of the sample, but 46.4% were not satisfied with how complaints were dealt with. This dissatisfaction could be associated with the later response that 78.6% of the young people felt that the scheme did not always find out who really committed the crimes. In addition 42.9% of respondents felt that offenders were not dealt with fairly, yet 82.1% of the young people viewed CRJ as being better than punishment beatings (see Table 3.8). Worryingly, this would suggest that a minority of young people see punishment beatings as a preferred method of disposal.

Table 3.8
Do you think it is better than punishment beatings?

		Frequency	Percent	Valid Percent	Cumulative Percent
Valid	yes	23	82.1	82.1	82.1
	no	5	17.9	17.9	100.0
	Total	28	100.0	100.0	

3.3 Volunteers' Perspectives

At the outset, CRJ volunteers were very anxious not to 'bias' the findings of the research, and wished to have an independent view of their work from the various cohorts interviewed in the study. Therefore, they distanced themselves somewhat from the process of gathering views. The CRJ currently has nine active male volunteers within a wide age range from early/mid 20s to mid 50s. The scheme does however have a larger pool of volunteers who have chosen to take a less active role, as a result of concerns about factors described above, related to the identity of the scheme.

This section is based on one relatively short focus group interview with four volunteers and one individual interview with the key volunteer. However, numerous informal discussions between researchers and volunteers took place at the researchers' request over the period of the study. Volunteers were understandably concerned with the outcome of the study, and anxious that it would be useful in improving the scheme and in helping to secure the funding to do so. Researchers found all volunteers to be co-operative and open and frank in their discussions, and helpful in facilitating the researchers to conduct the work.

A draft of this report was presented to the key volunteer, with a suggestion that he circulate it to other volunteers. Researchers also offered to meet all volunteers as a group, when they had read the final draft, to discuss the report in advance of the production of the final version. This is in recognition that it is perhaps the volunteers who have invested the majority of time and energy into Creggan CRJ, and we wished to respect this investment, by affording those who spent most time on CRJ to provide feedback on the report prior to finalising it. It was also an opportunity to iron out any errors which we have inevitably made as 'outsiders'.

Ultimately, the contents of the report and its main findings remain the responsibility of the researchers, and this does not mean that CRJ volunteers have agreed with all of the contents of the report.

The picture that emerged of the position of volunteers in the scheme pointed to a number of issues experienced by volunteers. These were low morale, overwork, issues about recruitment, supervision, support and training, the nature of the work and ownership of the scheme.

Low Morale

Throughout the period of time spent with the CRJ scheme it became evident that the scheme was highly dependent upon the reputation, determination, time and commitment of one volunteer in particular. This volunteer has been referred to as 'the key volunteer'. The other volunteers in the scheme unanimously confirmed this observation. As already stated, four of the nine volunteers took part in a focus group discussion with the researchers. The volunteers who were interviewed valued and admired the dedication of the key volunteer, and saw him as fully committed to the success of the scheme. However, they felt that his commitment and their own, was not matched outside a small pool of volunteers and a few supporters, and that the scheme had little support from the community. This perceived lack of support contributed greatly to low morale among the volunteers, whose morale was worryingly low, as manifested by remarks like "*why bother*" or "*we can't win*". Several volunteers also admitted that at times they questioned the sanity of their involvement with CRJ: "*...sometimes...I question myself, what the hell am I working for?*". Overall, all volunteers reported very low levels of morale. This could be related to a particularly difficult incident that occurred just prior to the focus group interview, and it is possible that, had volunteers been interviewed at another time, morale would have been higher. However, if this was the case, it is a matter of concern that one incident or crisis can reduce volunteer morale to the low level observed by the researchers. In our view, a CRJ scheme is difficult to sustain with such a low morale among volunteers, and methods of addressing this problem are urgently required.

Overwork

This low level of morale was compounded by the volunteers' sense that there was only a small number of volunteers to carry out a wide range of tasks. They experienced the pressure of incoming complaints and requests for their intervention, and felt overworked. They seemed to have reached the point where they were having difficulty in finding sufficient motivation in continuing with the work. The key volunteer was seen to be driving the scheme, and given the low level of morale and doubts expressed by the other volunteers, the researchers became concerned that since he was trying to motivate all the volunteers in addition to working on the scheme, that he was in danger of burnout. In the individual interview with the key volunteer, he admitted to having been close to this state on previous occasions. "*There's no question that I have been close to that on occasions...very, very close to it...*". Again, this is a matter of grave concern, and a central issue in the continued viability of the scheme.

Volunteers felt that improved recognition of their work by the community would be a major factor in improving motivation. The key volunteer agreed with this assessment: *"it would be an absolutely massive booster for these guys on the street here to see somebody else is interested"*. This would indicate an urgent need to develop a structure within the scheme, which would decrease workloads, provide support for volunteers, improve levels of community ownership and boost morale among the dedicated volunteers. In section 5 a suggested structure which could achieve these goals is outlined.

Recruitment of Volunteers

Volunteers felt that there was a need for more volunteers, in order to help decrease the workload. However, the existing volunteers perceived the chances of successfully recruiting suitable volunteers as slim, unless mechanisms were first put in place to facilitate and encourage community ownership of the scheme. Volunteers thought that community understanding of the nature and goals of the scheme had to be increased first, before people in the community would be prepared to support the scheme. However, volunteers felt that the task of increasing the level of understanding was impeded by the restrictions placed on them by principles of confidentiality: *"sometimes we are quite unpopular because of what we do. It's the greater good. The community doesn't really know you've solved it, because of the confidentiality situation. And the people you have worked with to solve it may not like the result! Then you are not very popular"*.

Incentives, such as payment, were suggested as a way of encouraging involvement in the scheme. However, some volunteers worried that this would mean that individuals would get involved for the wrong reasons and not for the good or benefit of the community. The key volunteer stated that *"once there would be paid jobs here there, would be problems...then it's perceived as, 'Ah well, you're doing it because you are paid!' you are not doing it because you want to do it, because you care"*. Whilst the notion of voluntary service is undoubtedly valuable, it might be important to revisit this issue in the future, with a view to developing a realistic policy about providing a sustainable service that is capable of meeting the needs of the community, without damaging the health of volunteers.

Support and Ownership

Another method of addressing the difficulties faced by volunteers is by improving the levels and sources of support that they experience. The volunteers also felt that a lack of support for the scheme existed among parents. This perceived lack of parental support upset and frustrated the volunteers, who saw the scheme's aims as ultimately to benefit families in the community, parents, as well as children, who, in the absence of CRJ may be subject to other forms of punishments such as beatings. This was compounded by volunteers' awareness of some of the social problems that lay behind the work that they did. Parental appreciation, therefore, might not be a reliable source of support for volunteers. One volunteer had concluded that, *"the parents just do not care"*. This observation was supported by a similar observation by the young people interviewed, who pointed out that CRJ could only work with the young people whose parents *'cared'* and who could support the principles of the scheme and ensure that the young person followed through the undertakings given in mediation. This was also compounded by the experience of some volunteers of being criticised themselves for their involvement in the scheme, and their children experienced taunting and name calling from the community, as a result of their parent's involvement in CRJ.

Volunteers were also frustrated with the lack of community ownership of the scheme, which led, in their view to the onus being on the volunteers to take the initiative and introduce new ideas or improvements. This perceived lack of ownership was viewed as problematic among the volunteers who now felt disillusioned and weary in their attempts to encourage community involvement, *"we haven't motivated the community…I went down and led a clean up…in the hope that it would motivate local people…it didn't happen"*. It would be important for the future development of the scheme that personnel, other than the volunteers, critically assessed past attempts at community involvement and found new and more successful approaches to encouraging community involvement.

The Nature of Work

Volunteers described serious difficulties in maintaining their motivation in the fact of the challenges that faced them. Chief among these difficulties was the sense of failure and disappointment of seeing some of their younger 'clients' re-offend. Whilst the CRJ work might be effective in some situations, the volunteers described that the scheme was *"not effective with all"* with certain categories of complaint. The low morale of the volunteers was undoubtedly associated with the feeling of ineffectiveness, combined with the sense that their work was not appreciated. The work involves going into difficult situations that people would usually go out of their way to avoid in order to maintain a quality of life. Yet volunteers who undertook to do this work were not only failing to be appreciated, but were being blamed and castigated for undertaking the work.

Time Commitment and Hours of Work

The key volunteer within the scheme also felt that the high level of time commitment required from the volunteers contributed to morale problems. *"The problem is one of time and commitment...and we generally end up with three to four on every given night...but I do most of the walking (to houses)"*. The volunteers described the hours worked as unsociable and, in addition, had a sense of being 'on duty' at all times. This has implications for volunteer support structures and schedules for working such as rotas. A further set of issues arises for volunteers who live in the community, who are 'tortured' with constant complaints, or who are continually accessible to those with whom they have been mediating. Clear boundaries between on and off duty are central in preventing burnout and in improving accountability in these circumstances. No doubt these difficulties have contributed to the conclusion reached by some volunteers, that the work is *"not attractive"*.

The volunteers have to deal with a considerable volume of complaints, all of a varied nature. However, some volunteers expressed frustration at some of the 'petty' and 'trivial' complaints being made, all of which have to be dealt with thus taking up more time. Some method of centrally receiving complaints and filtering out trivial complains before they reach volunteers would go some way to resolving this problem. However, this would imply the provision of a normal and an out of hours office staffed by trained staff capable of making such judgements.

Training and Supervision

The situations that are being dealt with by the volunteers are often highly complex, and fraught with difficulties. Although training is currently provided for all volunteers through NIACRO, some of the volunteers felt that some situations required more intensive or specialised training, perhaps on an ongoing basis. Current volunteers have had substantial experience of working in the Creggan community, a community which has faced many particular difficulties through the Troubles and through the multiple social problems of the area. For many years volunteers' work has not been supported and during those years, many have developed their own practice wisdom and methods to solve problems. Sometimes, training from a professional agency without a track record in the community can seem condescending to those who have had to make do and learn by discovery and trial and error. As a result, training needs to be tailored to the local needs in order to be useful and respectful of the volunteers' previous experience in the field. This background of the years of experience held by the volunteers was recognised by the leader, *"...somebody who has come through all those years, done all this work on the street and now being asked to go to meetings"*. For some volunteers, the way in which training has been offered in the past may have set up a certain degree of resistance to 'attending courses'. Courses should be delivered by individuals with a substantial amount of credibility in the eyes of the volunteers, otherwise training may come to be regarded as irrelevant or worthless. This must be avoided at all costs. Trainers must succeed in engaging the interest and commitment of local volunteers in order to improve morale and levels of support for CRJ work in the area.

The volunteers require supervision and support. Current supervision arrangements are limited and delivered on an ad hoc basis at a one-to-one level. Weekly meetings have been held but these may not be sufficient to meet the volunteer's needs. Given the level of stress involved in the work, and the level of difficulty and consequent risk to volunteers, it is of paramount importance that this situation is urgently reviewed. A more structured system of formal group support or supervision would be beneficial for all involved in the scheme. Currently the key volunteer, with little help, tries to motivate and encourage the whole team *"...mainly they (the volunteers) use me as a resource (of support) and I would either give that support or...if I don't have the skills we would bring in other people"*. However, this arrangement is not sustainable in the long term, and places an unbearable burden on the key volunteer, who attracts the concern of all participants in the scheme, as the overburdened role that he plays becomes more and more apparent.

3.4 Local Community Leaders' Perspectives

In this section, a range of leaders and local professionals were interviewed on their views and experiences of the Community Restorative Justice Scheme in Creggan. This data was collected in individual interviews and in a questionnaire survey of local teachers in one school. Those interviewed included a school principal, a local priest, a local community worker, and several local councillors from both Sinn Fein and the Social Democratic and Labour Party.

Teachers' Perspective

An individual interview was conducted with a principal in one of the local high schools in Creggan. In addition, 32 questionnaires were distributed to teachers to assess their opinions about the CRJ scheme both generally and in Creggan.

Individual interview with school principal

Behaviour

In this interview, the social problems experienced by young people in Creggan came across strongly. The principal explained how these problems were now manifest in the form of behavioural problems in the school. According to the principal, these problems, which can also be seen in the wider community, are associated with a lack of role models within the community for young people to base their behaviour upon, *"They have very few role models for what is loosely termed acceptable behaviour"*. Consequently, in his view, standards of behaviour have been deteriorating over the years and schools are now experiencing difficulties in managing behaviour, *"We are finding that youngsters now are coming through primary school with behaviour which would only have manifested itself in a school like this ten/fifteen years ago at about year 9, 10, 11 going on towards year 12…"*. The principal thought that these problems were symptomatic of what was going on in the wider community.

Paramilitary Influence

Although these problems may also be found in many schools throughout Northern Ireland, in Creggan both pupils and teachers have had to deal with the close proximity of paramilitaries within the community, *"the routine most days when this was a no-go area was …target practice [for the IRA]"*. This target practice was often held on the hill outside the school and, according to the principal, this exacerbated the situation.

Although these activities have since ceased, the school still bears the mark of past violence. Items recently confiscated from pupils could be associated with paramilitary activity, *"…when you have to go and take things like this and this from pupils, you know… it concerns me. It is a divers knife, they carry them because they are afraid"*. This fear was evident throughout the earlier discussions that the researchers held with the young people.

Relationship with the CRJ Scheme

The school principal in question admitted that the school had very little or no association with the CRJ scheme in Creggan. This is in spite of the fact that they are dealing with some of the same problems, and indeed probably the same children and young people: *"there is no connection between CRJ out there and the school here at all"*. However, the principal indicated that he would be willing to investigate the possibility of establishing and developing links with the scheme. Some of the young people might not be keen to have the school involved, according to the principal, as they would regard CRJ as 'their life outside school', *"some of the youngsters will see this as the school butting in on their outside lives, ... and they would get really annoyed ... they divorce what happens outside and what happens at home to what happens at school".* However, whilst the young people may not welcome better collaboration between school and community, it might make for a better CRJ scheme and a more effective containment of the difficult behaviour of some of the young people.

Dealing with Authority

The principal pointed out that there was a need to find more effective approaches when dealing with young people, as they do not respond to an authoritarian manner. He emphasised that it is important to establish a relationship with individual young people before problems can be dealt with: *"they have to see people like me being able to say hello to them, to have a laugh",* before dealing with difficult issues such as their behaviour. The relationships established also need to extend to families, *"it's very much families that we deal with".* The lessons learned in the school could be of potential benefit to the CRJ scheme if communication between the scheme and the school was developed.

Questionnaire

The questionnaire assessed the views and opinions of the teachers towards the CRJ scheme. Thirty-two teachers responded. Over 90% (90.6%) of the respondents defined CRJ as "a non-violent way of dealing with law and order problems in the community" with 9.4% seeing is as 'a way of getting people to pay for their crimes'.

The success of CRJ was also evaluated (table 3.9) with over half of the respondents (59.4%) indicating that they felt 'it works OK with minor crimes but is no use for violence or things like rape'. This is also how the CRJ volunteers and organisers view the schemes established in all areas of Northern Ireland. 21.9% also felt that the scheme works for offenders but not victims, indicating that these respondents felt that the scheme did not provide victims with a sense of justice having been done.

Table 3.9

Opinion of CRJ	Frequency (N=32)	Percent
It works OK with minor crimes but is no use for violence or things like rape	19	59.4
It works for the offender but not the victim	7	21.9
It has no real effect on crime levels in the community	3	9.4
Don't know	5	15.6

Respondents were also asked if they felt that CRJ was a good idea, and over half (59.4%) indicated that they felt 'it was a good idea that local people run schemes to deal locally with local problems'. As stated elsewhere, although local people are involved to some extent in the Creggan scheme, increased involvement and a more formalised management structure composed of local community leaders and representatives might be worth considering as a way forward for the Creggan CRJ. 21.9% felt that the CRJ was a good system 'until we get a proper police force' indicating that for some people, the scheme is only viewed as an interim approach. A small minority (9.4%) felt that the scheme would be 'OK or better if the police were involved'. This suggestion is unlikely to be made by many in Nationalist/Republican areas due to that community's attitudes to the police. Some teachers also added that there was a need for more communication with statutory agencies such as the Social Services.

The majority of the teachers felt that CRJ had problems, with only 3.1% saying that there were no problems at all. Table 3.10 illustrates responses on perceived problems, with 50% of the teachers indicating that the main problem in their view was that 'it can't deal with serious crime'.

Table 3.10

Problems with CRJ	Frequency (N=32)	Percent
No problems	1	3.1
It is not a deterrent to crime	8	25.0
It does not satisfy victims of crime	9	28.1
It rewards wrongdoing	2	6.3
It is run by the wrong people	3	9.4
It is in competition with the legitimate police force	1	3.1
It can't deal with serious crime	16	50.0

Other problems were identified by the teachers were a lack of awareness among the community of the CRJ scheme, and the scheme not being run or organised properly.

The teachers also suggested improvements to the scheme. The majority (59.4%) indicated that they felt that there was a need to make the scheme better known. In the light of the interview with the principal, it is not surprising that teachers are suggesting that the scheme should be better known, since there are no formal associations between the school and the scheme. 18.8% of the teachers also felt that the penalties within the scheme for offences ought to be tougher. Other suggestions included letting victims and offenders have involvement in the scheme, getting an independent body to run the scheme and the circulation of information in local schools aimed at informing teens and older primary school children about how and why the scheme operates.

Overall, the majority of teacher respondents (65.6%) felt that the CRJ scheme was a better alternative to punishment beatings, in spite of the problems they identified with the scheme. However, responses from the teachers indicated that they thought that changes were necessary within the Creggan scheme in order to ensure more successful outcomes.

The Priest's Perspective

When CRJ was being developed in Creggan, local community leaders were approached for guidance and support. The priest in the area was initially involved in these meetings but since this, has had little direct involvement with the scheme. He was interviewed about his perceptions of the problems in the area and the role of the scheme in addressing these.

Problems and Concerns with the Scheme

The priest revealed that his initial involvement was prompted by concern about the 'integrity' of the scheme, *"The first concern I would have had was the integrity of it all. Is this as it seems or is it simply a front for someone else?... My involvement over the first six months or so, going to a few meetings was to try and really ascertain who was involved, whether this project stood on its own"*. These meetings and his current knowledge of the scheme have led his attitude of being *"fairly happy"* about the scheme as the CRJ are *"not from some political or politically motivated initiative but has come about as a result of a need that was identified within the community"*. Thus the priest had satisfied his early concerns about the scheme and lessened his involvement as a result.

Experiences of the CRJ volunteers at 'work' have been positive,

"...my experience of seeing them operate from here on the ground has been, and certainly from the times where I have tried to involve them in situations I have felt, that they have tried to deal with them [young people] in an honest manner. And there's been a genuine concern about the young people, say, who have been the offenders...to get help for them".

The priest felt that his initial concerns were now alleviated and the scheme was trying to help the community but that certain problems still continued to exist. These problems were: the small numbers of volunteers involved; and the enormity of their workload; and the adequacy of their training:

"My experience of it as to how its panned out here over the last couple of years would be certainly, a small group of people putting a huge amount of effort into making themselves available and trying to deal with the various problems that arise. And I have on a number of occasions said that, you know, that there's a need to try and broaden out the base here because there's a danger of burnout. You have a small core of people who are being called upon by all sorts of different people to deal with all sorts of different problems. And because they are voluntary, they had a minimum of training. And that's my fear, that somehow or other they just won't be able to cope with the volume of work that's put their way".

The priest also felt that the whole scheme was being driven by one individual who *"was carrying the whole weight on his shoulders"*. The priest suggested that this "weight" could be lightened if proper structures were put in place, *"It is an enormous amount of work, because there are very little structures involved"*.

The priest also felt that there was pressure placed on volunteers to ensure the process of CRJ was successful among young people, and when it wasn't successful tensions arose. *"There's still tension, that if someone proves to be such a difficult problem and Community Restorative Model isn't working with them, you know, what's the next step?"*. The implication of this comment is that a lot is at stake in the scheme. If the non-violent methods are perceived in the wider community as a failure or as ineffective, then will that increase the demand for violent methods?

Violence in the community

This 'next step' the priest referred to has very often been violent in the form of punishment beatings. In the priest's view, the community accepted and tolerated violence:

"There's a tolerance for violence, I mean…the threshold has been lowered so much now that it's seen as an acceptable way of dealing with problems. And to either expel someone or to give them a beating, that's seen as a natural way of meeting their justice. While people, when they come face to face with it, might feel repulsed, at the end of the day many people will sort of shrug their shoulders and say, you know, 'That's the way - if you behave that way!' And there is an acceptance, there's a passive acceptance that this is the way to deal with this. which gives an indication …of how there's an acceptability of violence".

However, in the view of the priest, CRJ had provided an effective challenge to these attitudes and to support for this kind of violent behaviour, *"CRJ has challenged that [beatings] and also challenged the results of it all"*.

Perceptions

Like others in positions of leadership within the community, the priest felt that it was essential for locals to be involved in the scheme. However, this was not a straightforward matter, and he worried that community perceptions about possible 'offenders' might get in the way of those offenders getting a fair and just 'hearing'.

"I suppose they may feel, for instance, that the person involved from CRJ has a certain perception of them and their family. And, you know, they can't get beyond that. So that can sometimes be a

problem, yes. And also, you know, as I've said already, there's small, small core of people involved. Others may be in some way enlisted, but they might have the minimum of training. And when you go into a situation where there is a lot of tension and maybe where there is a lot of anger, it requires a certain type of person to be able to handle all of that, without it sort of spilling over".

So the priest recognised the complexity of the work within CRJ and the high level of skill required in a CRJ volunteer. He felt that Creggan scheme could make some changes in order to achieve a better standard of CRJ practice.

Improvements Required within the Scheme

The first step, in the priest's view was establishing a *"broader ownership of CRJ"* within the community. He considered the idea of a community charter worthwhile in helping to achieve this and involve the community more:

"I think if, first of all, there was a broader ownership of CRJ. One of the ideas which had been floated a while back by [name of individual] and others was some kind of charter, that there would be a kind of community charter which would be publicised and it would be, it would really be a charter which would communicate a few basic I suppose standards that, you know, would be, things that would be tolerated and wouldn't be tolerated in the community. I think it was going to be phrased in quite a positive sense rather than sort of ten commandments of 'thou shalt not'. But it was a certain charter that was going be publicised. And the idea would be sent around the homes. And in some way or another a method would be devised whereby we would try to get the consent of the community for this charter. I think that that would be a big help because it would mean then that the idea of restorative justice isn't just the initiative of either a few do-gooders or a few people who are political representatives but that the community in some way would recognise the need for it. If that was done, in a sense the idea of having it in a broader base, then you might encourage others to get involved, for instance, from schools and people locally".

The priest also thought that more training should be available for volunteers. *"What CRJ needs by way of training...I think a lot of it would be just in the whole area of dealing in conflict situations, what your role is there, what are the limitations, maybe learning from example elsewhere. I know that we had someone speaking to us from, a guy from South Africa came over. But I think there's a need just for a basic kind of understanding of what role you can play in going into to try and mediate between people, those kind of basic skills..."*

He also suggested that the whole structure of the scheme should be altered to ensure responsibility was shared among a wider cohort of people and to develop a larger sense of accountability,

"I suppose my own impression from here would be that it's really trying to broaden it out in such a way that the burden does not fall on a few people's shoulders, that there's some kind of structure there. And also that CRJ in turn has got some kind of accountability, that there's a forum there whereby those involved are accountable. Because at present, you know, that's probably a lack within the organisation in how accountable are they in turn, to the community".

He also suggested that obtaining some form of broad-based 'endorsement /recognition' of the scheme would be a way of motivating and encouraging volunteers:

"I suppose the endorsement of CRJ by political groups. I think if we had some sort of recognition of it…I think if it was seen to be broader based then it might have a better chance of being effective".

Anti-social Behaviour

Anti-social behaviour in the community has been largely blamed on young people, especially young males in the view of the priest. He recognised that a large number of the complaints received by CRJ were about young males in the community, *"for whatever reason it seems that the bulk of problems are generated from that age group and they are adolescent male"*. This behaviour on the part of the young males, he felt, was a result of their low self-esteem:

"In an area like this - and I'm not saying it's by any means unique to the Creggan - there seems to be, among young lads, a lack of …a poor self-esteem, very poor self-image. And a lot of cases they don't see themselves as being of any great worth or value. That all breeds a certain kind of sub-culture which very often degenerates into destructive behaviour".

Like the school principal, the priest thought that the behavioural problems could be associated with the lack of appropriate role models within the community for young people, *"They are also learning some of their behaviour from the older male generation, you know, 20's, 30's plus, where there are a lot of problems…so I think it's happening in the male population in general".*

Efforts within the community had been made to curb anti-social behaviour but these efforts have not always been successful, in his view:

"Well, I mean, there are, and I'm sure if you, especially if you speak to the schools they would be able to tell you about, you know, various initiatives that have been tried out, even through schools, or through youth clubs, you know, to try and do precisely what you say, to try and prevent young fellas getting to the problem stage. I wouldn't, I'd say it hasn't been through any lack of effort".

According to the priest, this lack of previous success has led those delivering such programmes to become frustrated with the situation and at times 'give up' on the programmes initiated. This, however, is to the detriment of the entire community, and schemes aimed at positive intervention on this issue are badly needed.

Local Councillors' and Community Workers' Perspectives

The final cohort of interviewees was composed of local councillors and community workers. They were interviewed individually about their views and experience of CRJ in Creggan. Their responses are analysed and presented together.

Successes and Failures of the Scheme

Perceptions of the effectiveness of the scheme varied. Some interviewees felt that it attempted to deal with anti-social behaviour and on many occasions succeeded in reducing this behaviour. These interviewees generally felt that the CRJ were *"doing excellent work"*. However, some were less supportive, seeing the scheme as narrow in its remit, because it dealt mainly with young male adolescents and not the wider community. *"What they have in place is some kind of project which looks at anti-social behaviour, by mainly young people and specifically young men…not broader issues"*. It was also suggested that the CRJ were *"doing a reasonable job"* but their job was being made more difficult because of the 'alienation' of young people from CRJ.

A perceived failure of the scheme by some of these interviewees was that young people viewed the CRJ as being the step before a possible punishment beating, *"My perception is that…CRJ scheme is a way of warning them and if they don't do as they are told in it the next step is like punishment beatings down the line"*. Thus, according to one interviewee, there was an implied threat to young people, whether intended or not by CRJ volunteers, *"There is an implied threat of violence, either perceived by the young people, or actually there"*.

Some interviewees also reported a degree of confusion among the young people about the differentiation between the CRJ volunteers and those involved in punishment beatings, *"In the minds of the young people in Creggan, there isn't any difference between the people who* are operating the scheme and those who are carrying out the punishment beatings". This was perceived by one interviewee to be a serious problem that required addressing. Some interviewees also felt that the current scheme 'fails' young people in some ways. This failure was due to the scheme not having preventative measures in place to prevent anti-social behaviour from occurring in the first place, "They don't have a clear idea of looking behind behaviour …prevention rather than reprimanding …".

Implicit in the comment was a call for a more therapeutic approach to the offender – an approach, which may not sit well with all offenders, particularly those interviewed who eschewed 'getting a talking to'.

The scheme's current approach relies on the idea that reprimands are effective, and is based on the premise that these will be effective in preventing a reoccurrence of offending behaviour. This interviewee suggested that this procedure relies on 'naming and shaming' which further excludes young people from the community, "The scheme brings victims and perpetrators together…and try to find a way forward…together with naming and shaming". This was felt to be a problem with the scheme, and that the scheme should rather be trying to prevent anti-social behaviour, and assessing why young people behave as they do within the community, "look at what is behind the behaviour as well as the actual behaviour".

Improvements Required Within the Scheme

A number of interviewees were strong supporters of the scheme, and able to point to CRJ's successes, they also identified areas for improvement. One interviewee felt that the scheme was not "perfect at the moment due to lack of volunteers" but that it would eventually work better, but this was going to require "a lot of time and money". It was also felt that the scheme required more help, "need more people on board – more of the parents and young people themselves". Encouraging more community involvement, was also seen as a further improvement for the future. "There has to be a bigger involvement by everyone."

Some interviewees indicated that the focus had to be on preventative measures, but this focus would require a greater understanding of young people within the community. "There needs to be a fundamental change in how young people are seen and that only can happen if people talk and listen to young people". The position of young people in the broader society led one respondent to the conclusion that substantial social change was necessary to solve the problems faced by communities such as Creggan. "Society needs a far better approach to deal with those issues [alcohol and drugs] and there are issues which the older generation do not understand".

Perceived Need for the scheme

Some of those interviewed felt that there was a need for the scheme due to the lack of viable existing alternatives. The issue of the police force (RUC) was raised as well as the current punishment beatings, *"No alternative as people do not recognise the RUC and more and more people are sending for them"; "It [CRJ] arises here because we do not have 'normal' policing ... other forms of punishment are being used and CRJ are attempting to replace that"* and *"For nationalist areas there would never, until such time we have community policeman, be RUC involvement".*

However, one interviewee felt that although CRJ is generally viewed as 'an alternative to policing,' the CRJ in Creggan was fulfilling this role. This was because their focus on young people's behaviour resulted in a narrowing of the range of issues CRJ dealt with, *"CRJ in the Creggan is not an alternative to policing because it does not look at other issues".* It was felt by some of the interviewees that although the scheme is perceived as only dealing with anti-social behaviour that it has the potential to *"be more than that".*

Remit of the scheme and training

Information from this cohort of interviewees was contradictory. Some held the view that only anti-social behaviour was dealt with and others saw CRJ as involved in a wider range of issues. Some of the issues that CRJ were asked to deal with were outside their remit, according to others: *"There are areas we can't handle ... outside our remit".* These issues include the more serious crimes such as abuse and rape – they are passed on to Social Services. Training was seen as a way to improve volunteers' capacity to handle these issues and know where to seek help and advice from the appropriate agencies, so that serious cases could be appropriately dealt with.

"CRJ has been approached on a range of issues... they have been asked to be involved in issues that range very widely - child protection issues and domestic violence. They have sought training from NIACRO and other sources to advise their people and enable their people to handle that ... which is not to investigate or be the agency that deals with that but properly refer".

3.5 Victims' perspectives

In order to ascertain victims' perspectives on the Creggan CRJ scheme, five interviews were conducted with victims identified by CRJ volunteers. These victims were asked to participate by the volunteers, who selected them, and sought their consent. They were then contacted independently and interviewed by Damien McIlory from St Columb's Park House. Transcripts of interviews were then analysed by ICR staff.

Interviews with victims collected data in five key areas:

1. Understanding the CRJ scheme: What is Community Restorative Justice? How would you define it?

2. Approval of the CRJ scheme: How well does Community Restorative Justice work? Do you think that CRJ is a good idea? Do you agree with it?

3. Experience of the CRJ scheme: Could you describe the process of the CRJ scheme?

4. Feelings before/after the CRJ process: How did being involved in a CRJ scheme help you with your feelings about what happened to you?

5. Improvements and changes of CRJ: From your involvement in the scheme, do you have any complaints about the CRJ process? What are they?

Each area will be discussed in turn.

3.5.1. Understanding the CRJ scheme: What is Community Restorative Justice? How would you define it?

Responses from victims about their understanding of Community Restorative Justice revealed a rather mixed set of impressions of the role and purpose of CRJ. In case A, the victim regarded CRJ as effective:

"It worked very well for us in Rinmore Drive because there was drinkers on the street. When they were approached they stopped - and were allowed back onto the street again, but I wasn't too happy about it. It worked better because when they where allowed back onto the street they stopped the drinking and the noise at night. When I passed them they spoke to me and we got on really well - we had conversations with one another, that's how I learned not to go out with a bad attitude towards them".

In this case, the victim implies that CRJ not only changed the perpetrators behaviour but the victim's 'bad attitude'. In case B, the victim saw CRJ as *"related to punishment beatings, better understanding, more talking to them than beating them - I agree with that. I think it is better".*

Case C saw CRJ more as, *"a support group, if you have a problem it will be solved, they are there to back you up. We do really need CRJ in the Creggan".*

Similarly case D, saw CRJ as supportive of them, but emphasised their impartiality and effectiveness:

"I know I have people I know I can call on and they're not panning me off – they're just telling me straight and fair. If I have a serious problem I can rest assured it will be sorted out for me".

Victims' understanding of CRJ seemed to be based on their direct experience of the operation of the CRJ scheme in Creggan, rather than on any grasp of overarching principles or information about CRJ from elsewhere. There was a perception on the part of some people that CRJ was there to support them, which presents a challenge to the impartial role that some other victims cast CRJ in.

Approval of the CRJ scheme: How well does Community Restorative Justice work? Do you think that CRJ is a good idea? Do you agree with it?

Victims were asked if they thought the CRJ scheme was effective. Responses were unanimously positive, with all victims reporting their support and appreciation of the scheme, and reporting no problems with it.

Case A: Its works very well - I agree with it!

Case B: I believe it works really well, makes a difference it is working here an makes a difference in Creggan - it is a good idea.

Q: Are there any problems with CRJ?

Case B: No problems

Case C: I do agree with it 100% especially for the children in the Creggan area. They (CRJ) do a lot for the children and for people in the community and a lot for people who have problems, I do agree with it totally.

Q: Are there any problems with CRJ?

Case C: Not that I know of, I've never had a problem, even though I spoke to them before and they had to go and sort it out - no I've never had any problems.

Case D: Very, very good idea - and I agree with it totally.

In one case, the interviewee reported that CRJ had worked when all other methods had failed. Interviewees also praised the hard work of the volunteers:

Q: Thinking back to your CRJ experience, was it a success?

A: A good success - if you went out to them, it didn't matter how many complaints, if it was 10 in the week they would deal with it and it always worked.

Whilst some of the positive attitude might be explained by the fact that CRJ volunteers selected the interviewees, nonetheless, the overwhelmingly positive attitudes of victims to CRJ was striking.

Interviewees compared CRJ positively to other methods of dealing with problems in the community.

Q: How does CRJ compare to other methods used?

A: Better understanding. If boys done anything wrong they were getting punishment beatings. I think it's working better for the boys and for those who intervene to stop them getting punishment beatings, support and understanding.

Experience of the CRJ scheme: Could you describe the process of the CRJ scheme?

Victims described their experiences of the scheme in some detail, illustrating how they had reached such positive conclusions about the scheme. The Case B interviewee gave an account of the multiple difficulties faced by the sons in his family, the trouble they had got into with local paramilitaries, the punishments they had received and how CRJ intervention affected the situation:

In 1970 I had one of my boys, when he was 15 he was put out of the country. The first boy [name] the RUC recruited him as a tout and they [IRA] could have shot him dead. They showed a bit of mercy by letting him go out of the town. I could have been down visiting him in the cemetery like my other son. After he was put out, my other two sons were taking all the stick. Children can be hurtful and spiteful to one another. Some things can hurt children. So they went on the wrong tracks. And my second son was put out of the town. He was out six years and my other son was just a wee hood. He done things he should not have done. Fortunately he was given a bit of leeway too. He was told to get out of the town and was let back in again. He was only back 24 hours and was breaking into places. CRJ came and told me he was back at his carry-on. If he had got a hiding he would have ended up in a wheel-chair. I believe the boys up here have nothing - only CRJ.

My son was out of town for 13 years from he was 15. My other son was 26 when he died. And the people I went to see let my son back into the town for the week of the funeral. And then he had to leave again. He told me he was going to do himself in. I was anxious and worried. And my other son was let out of jail for the funeral...

Q: Did you feel that CRJ was a success?

Yes. For me, the first time I approached to get my son back - but that wasn't it, the IRA gave me the answer, 'No.' The CRJ got involved. They came up and told me my son could come back and gave me the re-assurance to make me feel more secure and his wife more secure.

Q: Was it a failure in any way?

It was a success... So I was happier, and I got the re-assurance from these people here, after doing what I did do - putting it in the papers - it made me able to settle down...He was going to be all right here.

The interviewee in Case C typifies complaints received by CRJ as a result of disputes between neighbours. The interviewee described her problems, and how CRJ intervention affected the situation:

I had a neighbour giving me a lot of hassle, abuse, bad language. 2-3 am in the morning you were woke out of your sleep, we had a terrible bad experience with them....We went to the RUC to the Barracks, we had interviews with the police, we got them up when something next door actually happened, to be honest all we where getting was advice. We could have pushed for a summons but we really didn't want to do that, we got advice on how to handle it rather than how to get it stopped.

Q: Did CRJ resolve the problem?

It was a success, we went to see [name of volunteer]. We explained to him the problem and he gave us a time he would call to see us. He came to my home, sat down and we talked. I explained what ...was happening and the abuse that we where getting. He then went in and tried to solve the problem. He didn't take anyone's side and tried to solve the problem and he talked to the person. The support that you got when you went to [name of volunteer] or anyone else! They were there for you. It was a success, in our situation you needed support at a personal level. You can go and talk to anybody over there (CRJ). They solved the situation when it happened. They were great at that.

Case D was similarly about problems between neighbours, which was also successfully resolved,

The first time that I known about the CRJ was that I was unfortunate to have noisy neighbours. I'd tried to communicate civilly and justly and I just wasn't getting across, so I went to me local CRJ office. And within a few hours they were up at my home and we had a talk, discussed my problem and within 24-36 hours the problem was sorted out.

Case E also typified many referrals received by CRJ – a complaint about young people on the streets of the area,

Group of boys across the street, I felt they were harassing me, because when I went out they were calling names at me. [They] always called to us all the time. We couldn't go outside the door, they were always calling something. They fired everything - between eggs, apples from the apples tree that I had. And snowballs when the snow was there. Everything. Stones, you name it. They fired them at my windows, at the car and everything. I tried to talk to them. I stopped the car one time and they fired the snowballs at my face. But it didn't do any good. I went over to them when they were stealing the apples and I said to them [that] they could have them when they are ripe. But it didn't go any good. I don't know why, but they just keep on. And every time we went out - my husband went out - we went to the mobile (shop) - they called after us. And I just felt really, I was at the end of my tether! And I felt it was the only time that I ever wanted to move from this house. I felt I just didn't know what to do. .I don't believe in violence and I don't believe violence solves anything, so I did try to talk to them. I work with young people all the time and I talk to them. I know they have problems and I would try and speak to them in that way. But it was no good with this crowd. It just didn't work. My baby was really ill and I said to them, that I had a baby that was ill and that I just couldn't take it. I tried to reason with them but it just didn't work.

Q - How did you find out about CRJ?

I went to the priest and he said there was a group in Creggan, 'I can get in touch with them,' that he would get in touch with [local SDLP councillor]. And his words to me was, 'I don't know what this group do, but what ever they do it works!' That was the priest's words to me. So I said, 'OK. You can contact the group through the local councillor!'

So that night when my husband and I came back in, my son said the councillor was down looking for us, and he would be back down at 6pm, and we weren't going to be in. I had to work. So we went up and saw him. I would know the councillor to speak to now and again. I went up and told him we wouldn't be in, so he put us on the phone to [a CRJ volunteer] and we gave the names and he said he would see about it. We went. We came in that night and one of the parents arrived at the door with one of the boy's crying his eyes out. I said, 'Nothing has happened tonight, but this has been going on a long-time,' I told her. But she said "[Name] wasn't there! It wasn't him!' And I said, 'It was!' I've known this girl a long time, and that his father would kill him if he knew he was doing anything. I went to her door before Christmas and told her about the wee boy laughing, that I didn't know which of the sons it was, but I knew it was one of them. She tried to say her son was like another young fella. I said to her, 'I'm telling you now it was him.' He said, 'No, it wasn't me! I'm not taking the rap!' That I'd run after him etc. I said, 'Sure, I told you about that!' I said to her, 'If you don't believe me, come down when [grandson] is in, and he'll be able to tell you it was him.' I told her I didn't know much of her two wee boys, but I said our [name], my grandson pointed him out and told me which one he was, so that's how I knew it was him. Before they left the boy stopped crying, I said, 'I'm telling you now, it was you!' So away he went. His father came to the door one day to [name]. He said he would see to his son, but the boy said it wasn't him. We didn't have any bother since.

In Case E, the intervention of CRJ seems to have resolved a situation that, left to their own devices, the parties could not resolve. The witnessing of the complaint of the victim, the involvement of a neutral third party seems to have led to an effective resolution to the problem from the point of view of the victim.

3.5.4 *Feelings before/after the CRJ process: How did being involved in a CRJ scheme help you with your feelings about what happened to you?*

Victims were asked how they felt during the CRJ process and subsequently, and whether their involvement with CRJ assisted them to overcome their experience of victimisation. The Case A interviewee reported that the CRJ process required an attitude and behaviour change on the part of the victim:

It helped me to know not to go out with a bad attitude. The boys were told they where allowed back into the street - but warned not to drink. But we weren't too happy at the start. But they stopped the drinking and behaved very well.

Q - How do you feel?

A: I didn't think it was going to work ...when they came back into the street, in case they started drinking again and the late night noise. But this didn't happen. They behaved themselves - and we got on very well.

CRJ intervention in this case was successful in altering relationships between the parties to the dispute. This had consequences for the victim's feelings about the wider area and community.

Q - How did you feel before CRJ?

A: I felt there was no hope for the street. And I think it was the worst street in Creggan because they gathered here more than any other street. And I didn't think we were going to get it stopped.

Q - When you first went to CRJ, how did you feel?

A: Well, I had no idea they were going to do something about it, which they did. And it was a success.

The interviewee in case A had increased hope for the future of the area, and an improved attitude to the estate as a result of the experience of CRJ intervention. Part of this was due to increased skill on the part of the victim and learning about how to effectively handle nuisances in the community. The victim learned how to deal assertively with difficulties.

Q - In what way was the CRJ successful?

A: You can deal with things instead of flying off the handle in bad temper and have a bad attitude towards them in the street. To go in [with] a nice attitude, it does help.

Q - How did you feel about the consequences of the CRJ?

A: Excellent - it worked in the street and for the rest of Creggan. There's a lot of people approaching CRJ now. More safer in own home, I am here nearly 50 year. It's a family home. I did want a transfer, but I don't any more, because I have a boy of 12 and I wouldn't want to move him, and I wouldn't feel safe anywhere else. It feels if we have bodyguards around here, because they are so good to us.

This increased confidence in dealing with difficulties has led the victim to reinvest in the local community, rather than feeling driven to the extreme measure of leaving the family home and relocating elsewhere. Other victims reported feeling very angry at the situation they were in, and felt that CRJ helped to resolve the difficult situation and find new solutions to the problem. The interviewee in Case B reported the outcome of his experience of CRJ:

B: I got my son back and I can see him every week. CRJ is good, really good - best thing happened up around here in Creggan.

Case C reported similar levels of satisfaction with the sense of security and support that CRJ provided. CRJ provided an additional resource and a source of advice and ideas for neighbourhoods struggling with local problems:

C: Good satisfaction, [it's] good to be able to turn to [names of CRJ volunteers], that you could turn to them other than your other neighbours. They where also getting abuse (us together), so CRJ would come and talk to us together, either in my home or my neighbours home. Good satisfaction on how to handle the situation, what to ignore and what not to ignore, it was a great help.

CRJ were also seen as advocates with the authorities:

C: They are great, not just for my situation but for other situations. I had a few occasions I had to go over to [CRJ volunteer] about the Housing Executive. They are supportive with that also, as I had meeting with the Housing Executive. To me CRJ are well needed in this community.

The interviewee in Case D saw CRJ as a better option than the various authorities and powers, and as more helpful:

Q - Did you go to anyone before hand?

D: I did. I went to my local Housing Executive and they where totally arrogant and rude and was treated very, very badly. I felt they are people that should be there, as I am a tenant of their home, and felt very betrayed after 28 years - that they could do nothing for me.

Another victim had approached Sinn Féin for help, without success.

E: I went up twice to N - she was a friend of mine - N out of Sinn Féin. But I went up, because she was a friend of mine, and said to her. I said to her on two different occasions. But she was to sort something out. But from what I could see, she didn't do nothing. In fact, I don't know if Sinn Fein spoke to them or not, because they said to me, 'We aren't afraid of Sinn Féin!' So I was at the end of my tether at Christmas...

Q - your own personal experience, your own contact to try and resolve the issue with Sinn Fein - and your friend - this didn't work?

E: It didn't work it made no difference, but they still harassed me, [they] still fired things at the window. We had to sit with our blinds open every night in-case they where going to come to the door. I told them that was doubled glazed windows that I had. The man up the street told me he had a double-glazed window broke and it cost him £130 and my windows are far bigger than his. I said 'It would cost your families if you break the windows!' Didn't make any difference!

E's next attempt to get help with this situation was to lead indirectly to CRJ.

Q - Did you approach anybody else?

E: Before that I didn't know the names, I knew them, I knew a couple of their names but I didn't know all their names, so I tried to find out - to me there was no point in going to anybody until you knew the names. They where always standing over there every night. My husband ran after them on a couple of occasions - if he got them I don't know what he would have done, but I stopped him anyway. ...And so when I found out the names I didn't know what to do, but the girl over the street was chatting to me. And she said to me that she went to see the priest down at Ballymac - he was a friend of hers and he suggested that I go see our priest. So I went to the priest and he said, "What would you like to do?" And I said, 'I don't know.' I said I feel like moving house that I never wanted to move from Creggan. I came to Creggan when I was 11 months old, my mother's house is still there, my brother who lives in England is moving back to it. I have lived in Creggan - apart from a couple of times I lived in England - I lived in Creggan all my life. And I have been here 28 years in this house this October, and my oldest son was only a baby when he moved in. And I just don't want to leave, and I know the place, and I am happy and have good neighbours on either side of me. I've met quite a few people on the street, the younger ones I wouldn't. I don't know everybody; I just mind my own business too... I wouldn't know the younger ones.

This lack of connection with the younger generation, and antipathy between young people and adults was a source of difficulty that often led to CRJ intervention. Victims interviewed saw CRJ as more effective in dealing with their difficulties than the other agencies approached.

Several victims remarked on the methods used by CRJ, the importance of 'not having a bad attitude' and of behaving like 'gentlemen' or like 'adults' and have reported learning from this about how to overcome their sense of helplessness and develop their own methods of dealing with difficult situations.

Q - Why and how did CRJ help you?

Why? Was when I explained to them the problem that I had, they went and sorted the problem out - when they came back and told me, I felt that was the problem solved... They went in and talked as gentlemen, sat down and explained the situation from me to them and they got the problem sorted out.

Q - So they mediated?

Yes they did, with perfect results. It took two or three other occasions to get the problem talked about, it was a continual process.

Q - How you felt before you went to CRJ?

I felt very isolated, very frustrated as a person and I was pulling my hair out because I didn't know what to do. Then I went to my local CRJ and they were like heaven sent, they were in my home, had a cup of tea and talked, discussed it as adults. When we finished talking I felt that it was going to be sorted.

Victims valued the seriousness with which their complaints were attended to, and the way in which they were listened to by a third party.

D: ...they listen to me, I knew when I was talking to them they where listening to me and when leaving my home I felt a lot was lifted off my shoulders

Q - How did you feel about the consequences and the conclusions of CRJ?

Great organisation! That they listen to you, understand you. And you know when you're sitting talking, they don't pan you off. They take your feelings into their consideration.

Improvements and changes of CRJ: From your involvement in the scheme, do you have any complaints about the CRJ process? What are they?

Finally, victims interviewed were asked about improvements that they might wish to make to the scheme. Victims felt unanimously positive about the scheme, and could see little room for improvement.

A: No complaints! Very successful!

B: I have no complaints

C: No complaints what so ever with CRJ.

D: The only complaint is that we didn't have them soon enough. They make me feel as a person that they are there for us and it makes you feel safe and secure where I live.

E: Whatever the fellas in that CRJ group did, I didn't ask, but it works! ...I don't know what they said when they talked to those weans, but it must have worked.

Victims reported confidence in the scheme, and E indicated willingness to use the scheme again, should the need arise.

Q What did you get out of being involved with the CRJ scheme?

E: I felt relieved, hopefully this problem will never happen again but if it does I'll be back at CRJ.

Victims were also asked about general improvements that would alleviate the difficulties faced by the community and addressed by CRJ intervention. Several interviewees mentioned the need for facilities and provision for young people, and the lack of such provision as a cause of difficulties in the community.

Q: How would you improve the scheme?

A: Youth club - to get youths of the streets, need to get something more organised for them.

Q: What was the best thing about your experience with the CRJ scheme?

A: It got the boys of the streets, and got a community centre for them to keep them off the streets.

Case B reported similar views:

Q: How would you improve the scheme?

B: For the young boys - get a place for them, give them something to do to take them off the streets at night. It would be a good thing for the community.

Interviewee D felt that social provision and jobs were necessary for the young people.

Q: How would you improve the scheme?

D: Yes, for the young children, teenagers, as a parent of teenagers the boys and girls find it very frustrating - that is the only thing if they could work for the teenagers.

Q - In what way?

D: Like social clubs, places where they can go to have a game of snooker or just somewhere to sit and talk.

Finally, victims were asked about the positive aspects of their involvement with CRJ.

A: This estate needs something like that. It's a good estate but we still need this organisation for everybody and there's people sitting in the house and they have nobody and they don't realise what we have in the Creggan.

Another interviewee had a more personal gain to report.

Q: What was the best thing about your experience with the CRJ scheme?

B: Getting my son back into the town - nobody isn't going to say nothing to him, nobody makes him feel out of place. Peace to myself and I can live here in peace and knowing we are secure here.

Other interviewees thought that CRJ was not well enough known in the community and beyond and did not get enough recognition for their good work.

Q: How would you improve the scheme?

C: A huge improvement could be made! There are other situations like myself and other people [who] don't realise how good they are, more for the community not just children but adults also.

Another interviewee felt that CRJ should advertise themselves more:

Q - Do you have any complaints?

E: I can only speak from my experience and say no. But I really do feel that they [CRJ] need to get out more and advertise, put leaflets through peoples doors and all, and let the ordinary people in this area know that this service is out there for them.

Q: What was the best thing about your experience with the CRJ scheme?

C: The support that you get, no matter what the subject is, like housing. Or if you are having bother - should it be vandalism in the streets - they are there to support. They don't just listen, they do something about it.

Victims were asked about the best aspect of their experience of CRJ. The gains they reported were impressive, and substantial.

Q: What was the best thing about your experience with the CRJ scheme?

D: The results that I received. I was able to go and talk to them and they have all my problems all sorted out!

Another interviewee was asked:

Q - What was the best thing you experienced?

E: Peace of mind! I can open my blinds without fear of somebody throwing things or shouting things. Right now I have peace of mind...me and my family have peace of mind.

In conclusion, whilst there were a range of critical observations about the way the current CRJ scheme operates, there was a widespread recognition of the time and energy devoted to the scheme by the volunteers. There was an appreciation of the need within the community for some form of CRJ scheme to continue within the Creggan area. A lack of wider participation on the part of the community was identified as part of the problem with the scheme.

In the course of conducting this research, two local school principals, a priest and some local teachers and others indicated an interest in serving on a management committee for the scheme should one be set up. There were also several creative ideas about the adoption of a charter within the community, and a deal of concern about the welfare of the current batch of volunteers who were perceived to be over-stretched and under-rewarded. In the concluding sections of this report, these findings will be drawn together in a set of conclusions and recommendations, and a suggested plan for the way forward presented.

---

[1] *This was the view of one interviewee*

Section 4: Conclusions, recommendations and ideas for the future

This section draws together the findings from the previous section and suggests some recommendations and ideas for the future of the CRJ in Creggan. A model structure of the CRJ scheme is proposed in Figures 4.1, 4.2 and 4.3.

Feasibility of Model Structure
Resources required

In order to realise the model structure the following resources would be required:

- Motivated volunteer committee members;
- Interested local agencies;
- Volunteer mediators;
- External expertise in CRJ;
- Volunteer support workers;
- Paid staff;
- Premises/office;
- Drop in facilities;
- Expertise in supervision and support for workers and volunteers;
- Funding.

The availability of these resources will determine the feasibility of establishing a more effective CRJ scheme. In the course of our work, we have determined that some of these resources are readily available, whilst others remain to be secured.

Access to required resources

The availability of each of the identified resources required is discussed below:

- **Motivated volunteer committee members**

The research conducted with local representatives included a priest, two school principals (one primary school and one secondary school), several secondary school teachers and two political representatives. Those interviewed indicated a willingness to serve on a committee that would manage a CRJ scheme. From these cursory enquiries, it would appear that there is a high level of motivation amongst locally based professionals to offer voluntary service to the community in order to assist in addressing the problems faced by the community. We were unable to establish the level of interest among local adult residents, but young people we interviewed also indicated an interest in having an input to the management of a CRJ scheme. Clearly, proper information, recruitment and induction of committee members would be an important part of the work of establishing a scheme. However, it does seem as though there are suitable local personnel with a sufficient level of interest to begin the process of establishing a committee. It will be important that the work of establishing such a committee does not fall back on the shoulders of the current volunteer mediators, who are small in number and overwhelmed by their current roles and responsibilities. Perhaps one of the local community organisations, or a small *ad hoc* group composed of the people identified here as interested could begin the work of establishing a committee. In the light of other difficulties outlined elsewhere in relation to ownership of the scheme, it is crucial that this work is conducted by a group of people who are broadly composed, and not from one particular political persuasion. This would ensure that issues of ownership and trust do not continue to prove obstacles to the scheme's development.

- **Interested local agencies**

The two local schools that we visited both indicated an interest in the scheme, as did the local Catholic Church, and Creggan Neighbourhood Partnership, who indicated a willingness to consider deploying a worker to do follow-up work with the young people. Agencies outside the immediate community such as NIACRO also have an interest and an input to work in the area, together with the statutory agencies such as Education Welfare, Social Services and the Probation Board. Other voluntary agencies such as St Columb's Park House have also demonstrated an interest and support. Although we did not conduct a comprehensive survey of local agencies, initial indications show that there is a sufficient level of interest among agencies to ensure that an expanded CRJ scheme would enjoy the support of agencies active in the local area. However, in the light of experience in other communities, it is essential that ownership of the scheme is seen to rest within the community and voluntary sector and not with the statutory agencies. Elsewhere, we discuss some aspects of the legacy of the Troubles for communities such as Creggan, where it will be necessary to build new and trusting relationships with authority in general and statutory authority in particular. Since this work has not yet been completed, it is important that the community sector maintains its integrity so that it is in a strong position to embark on this work in partnership with the statutory sector. Therefore, local agencies should be involved. Respect for local autonomy or management and principles of working in partnership with communities are particularly important characteristics for such work. Should professionals from local agencies be involved on the management committee, it is recommended that consideration be given to the nature of their involvement and whether they are representative of agencies or whether they are involved in a personal capacity.

- **Volunteer mediators**

Currently, a team of local volunteer mediators is already established. Two main concerns arise about this team. First, the level of support available to the volunteers currently operating is entirely inadequate, and as a result, they currently experience substantial demoralisation and stress. Although volunteer mediators can be recruited in the local community, it is essential that any future scheme makes proper provision for support, supervision, ongoing training, recognition and reward of volunteers, otherwise this essential resource - a supply of local volunteers - will be depleted and wasted. Second, some of the current volunteers have had to 'take a back seat' because of difficulties in local perceptions of the identity of CRJ, and anxiety that the local scheme would be seen to be over-identified with one particular political party or interest. This is, again, wasteful of local resources and demoralising for all volunteers, who experience themselves as over-stretched, yet are unable to utilise all the volunteer resources available to them. Thus it appears that the availability of volunteers and the ability of CRJ Creggan to sustain a supply of volunteers is dependent on two other factors: the ability of the scheme to establish an independent and credible identity for itself; and the ability of the scheme managers to foster a sense of ownership of the scheme by the entire Creggan community.

- **External expertise in CRJ**

Access to external expertise on CRJ is clearly essential. External expertise is necessary to support the work in Creggan, and in order to provide stimulation and guidance for the development of this local work, together with some potential training input. However, Northern Ireland is a divided society, and the provision of expertise from outside the community poses a considerable challenge in terms of 'matching' such external expertise to the needs of the Creggan.

This challenge is manifest in a number of ways. First, CRJ schemes operating in Loyalist communities and those operating in Republican communities, whilst facing many of the same issues, operate under somewhat different conditions. Attitudes to the police and the judiciary vary between the two communities, as, in many cases, does the age structure and informal infrastructure within the community. Furthermore, some of the volunteers (and increasingly staff) involved in CRJ are ex-paramilitary prisoners, and this can pose a particular challenge to cross-community work between CRJ schemes. Finally, Creggan is located in a predominantly Catholic city in the North West where limited opportunities for cross-community endeavour have existed in the past. In addition, historically there has been an independence of spirit, a sense of the uniqueness of the situation in Derry Londonderry, with its proximity to the border with the Republic of Ireland, and its historic role in the political history of the state and the nation. This is compounded by a strong desire to avoid 'coat-tailing' on Belfast.

Thus, inappropriate offers of outside expertise may give rise to certain resistance on the part of the community, and this might further compound the difficulties of collaborative work within Northern Ireland. Therefore the challenge is to find sufficient expertise of a nature and from a location that is accessible and useful to workers in Creggan. It may be that international linkages will prove an important part of this provision. International linkages can be important for their educational value, and for their capacity to broaden discussion beyond local tried and tested methods. Such linkages also improve the incentives for participation in the work of the scheme, and can enhance the credibility and prestige of the scheme itself. Linkages with other societies coming out of a period of political upheaval, such as South Africa, would be particularly appropriate.

- **Volunteer support workers**

The proposed structure for the scheme contains a proposal for the recruitment and deployment of a second cohort of volunteers who would be engaged in support work. Unlike the volunteer mediators, whose role is in the immediacy of the complaint, mediation and resolution situation, these volunteers' work would begin after the mediation process is over. Their role would be in befriending victims, offenders and others involved in the CRJ mediation process, and offering them support, social contact and ongoing attention where it is required. Some of these volunteers might be recruited as peer support or as substitute mentors for young people, or as visitors for elderly victims, and so on. These volunteers would be supervised by paid workers and trained by external expertise and paid workers.

- **Paid staff**

Currently, Creggan CRJ have no full-time paid staff. Given the level of difficulty of the work, the complexity of the tasks involved in managing a CRJ scheme, and the volume of work experienced in Creggan, having full-time staff to carry out both the administrative and intervention aspects of the work is essential. It is important that these staff are recruited according to their expertise and qualifications in administration and CRJ practice, and that the highest standards of practice, including confidentiality and integrity are maintained. These staff would be accountable to the management committee, the chairperson of whom would liaise directly with the most senior member of staff. The role of the paid staff would be to create and maintain conditions under which the largely volunteer workforce of CRJ Creggan can operationalise the principles of CRJ in Creggan with the support of the community. Thus staff would perform a range of roles, from offering professional supervision and support, to organising training, managing premises, ensuring financial accountability, fund-raising, and ensuring that appropriate channels of information and accountability are functioning between the community, the management committee, the paid staff, volunteers and participants. These roles and functions are clearly too onerous for volunteers to fulfil, alongside the delivery of mediation to the community, although this is the current situation. In order to ensure a quality service to the community of Creggan, it is essential that paid staff relieve volunteers of these roles.

- **Premises/office**

Allied to the employment of staff, it will be necessary to provide a workplace for such staff, and a place where volunteers, management committee members and other partners can meet, work, and engage in the operations associated with CRJ. It is important that these premises are accessible to the community, and are seen as neutral politically.

- **Drop in facilities**

Given the volume of CRJ work emanating from local adolescents in Creggan, and given the nature of the dynamic between these adolescents and the rest of the community, a drop-in facility adjacent to the CRJ office but separate from it would be a valuable – if not essential provision for CRJ in Creggan. The existing youth club services Lower Creggan, and is under-utilised since the young people in Upper Creggan will not use it, due to territorial issues. The current provision in the Corned Beef Tin is not clearly established nor is its relationship with CRJ clear to all who use it. Furthermore, staffing of the current facility is on a voluntary basis, and access can be sporadic. The ownership of an accessible CRJ Drop-In would greatly enhance CRJ's capacity for preventative work, and for exerting positive social influence on the young people, against whom the majority of complaints are made. Such a facility would also allow relationship building between the various interest groups involved in CRJ to take place.

- **Expertise in supervision and support for workers and volunteers**

Given the challenging nature of work in CRJ, the level of expertise required to deal with some of the more difficult situations encountered in such work is considerable. The level of risk associated with some of the interventions, and the attendant stresses placed on workers and volunteers makes it is essential and of paramount importance that regular, expert and effective support, supervision and debriefing systems are established for all staff and volunteers. Furthermore, it must be a requirement that all staff and volunteers participate regularly in such supervision and in regular in-service training. Such supervision and support should be established at two main levels. First, within the Creggan scheme itself, there is a need for an on-site supervisor or CRJ manager, whose role would be to support staff and volunteers in their work with parties to mediation, and with other agencies. Secondly, this manager must, in turn, be professionally supervised by an outside agency contracted for this purpose by the management committee. This outside agency would report to the management committee, notifying them immediately of any serious concerns about staff welfare or performance, and would provide routine reports to the management committee on the supervisory work, with due regard to issues of confidentiality.

- **Funding**

Many of the resources outlined above depend on the procurement of substantial funding for Creggan CRJ. The development of an agreed proposal for the scheme, and implementation of the process of building support for and ownership of the scheme in the local community are important first steps in securing the financial resources required to support the CRJ work described here. Furthermore, a great deal of interest on the part of the authorities and of various donors in CRJ work would indicate that a well-designed proposal that attracts wide support within the Creggan community would be an attractive proposition for a range of funders and donors.

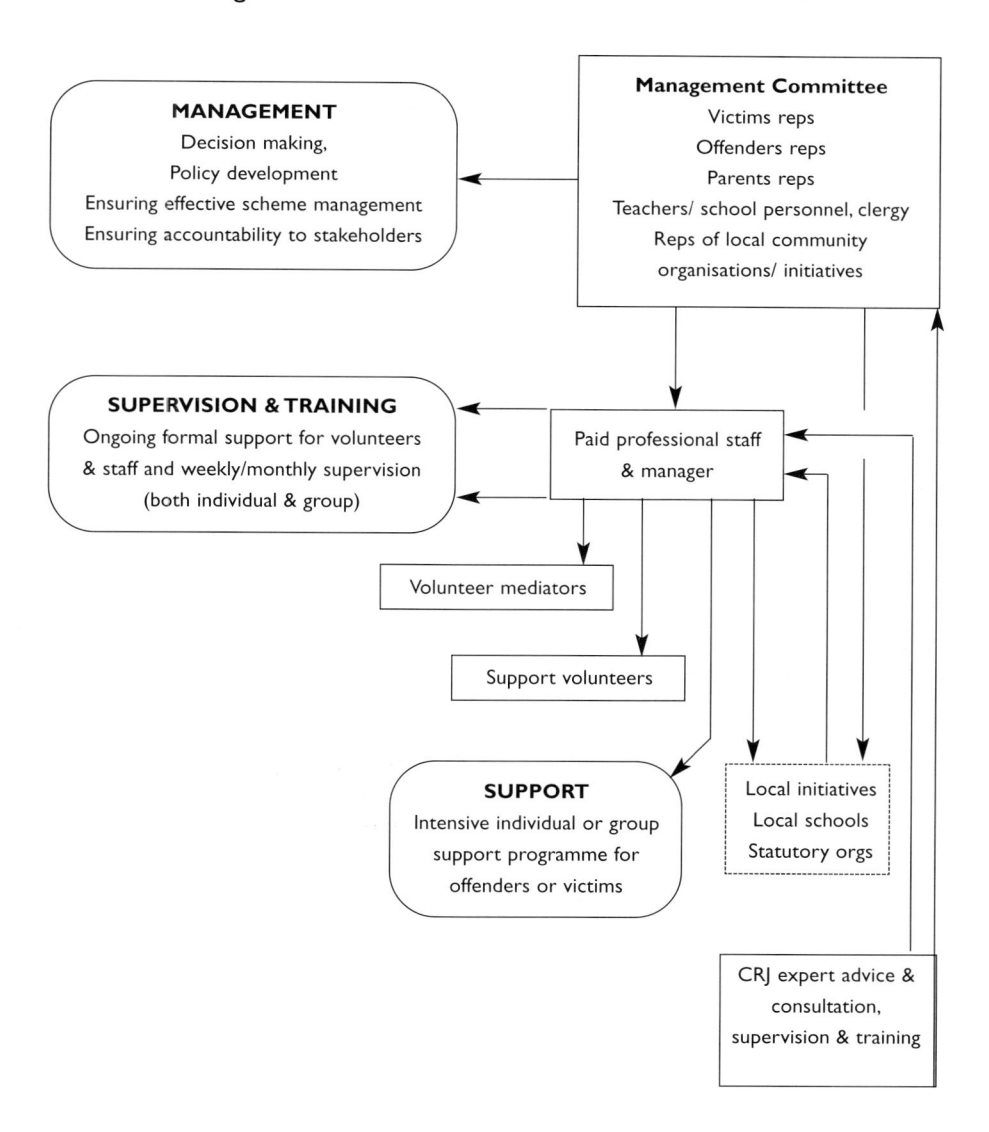

Figure 4.1 MODEL STRUCTURE FOR CREGGAN CRJ SCHEME - Management

MANAGEMENT
Decision making,
Policy development
Ensuring effective scheme management
Ensuring accountability to stakeholders

Management Committee
Victims reps
Offenders reps
Parents reps
Teachers/ school personnel, clergy
Reps of local community organisations/ initiatives

SUPERVISION & TRAINING
Ongoing formal support for volunteers & staff and weekly/monthly supervision (both individual & group)

Paid professional staff & manager

Volunteer mediators

Support volunteers

SUPPORT
Intensive individual or group support programme for offenders or victims

Local initiatives
Local schools
Statutory orgs

CRJ expert advice & consultation, supervision & training

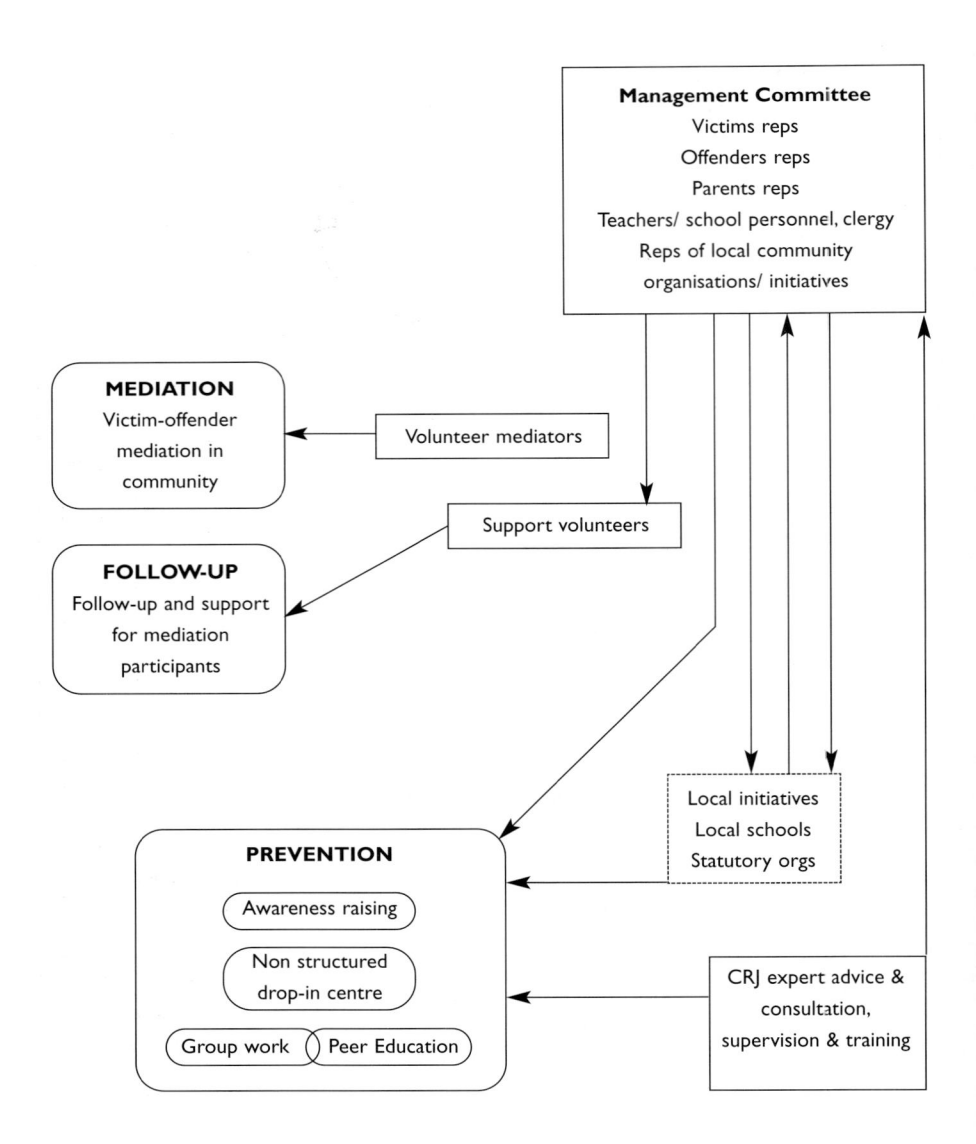

Figure 4.2 MODEL STRUCTURE FOR CREGGAN CRJ SCHEME - Services

Management Committee
Victims reps
Offenders reps
Parents reps
Teachers/ school personnel, clergy
Reps of local community
organisations/ initiatives

MEDIATION
Victim-offender mediation in community

Volunteer mediators

Support volunteers

FOLLOW-UP
Follow-up and support for mediation participants

Local initiatives
Local schools
Statutory orgs

PREVENTION
Awareness raising
Non structured drop-in centre
Group work   Peer Education

CRJ expert advice & consultation, supervision & training

**Figure 4.3 MODEL STRUCTURE FOR CREGGAN CRJ SCHEME -
Management and Services**

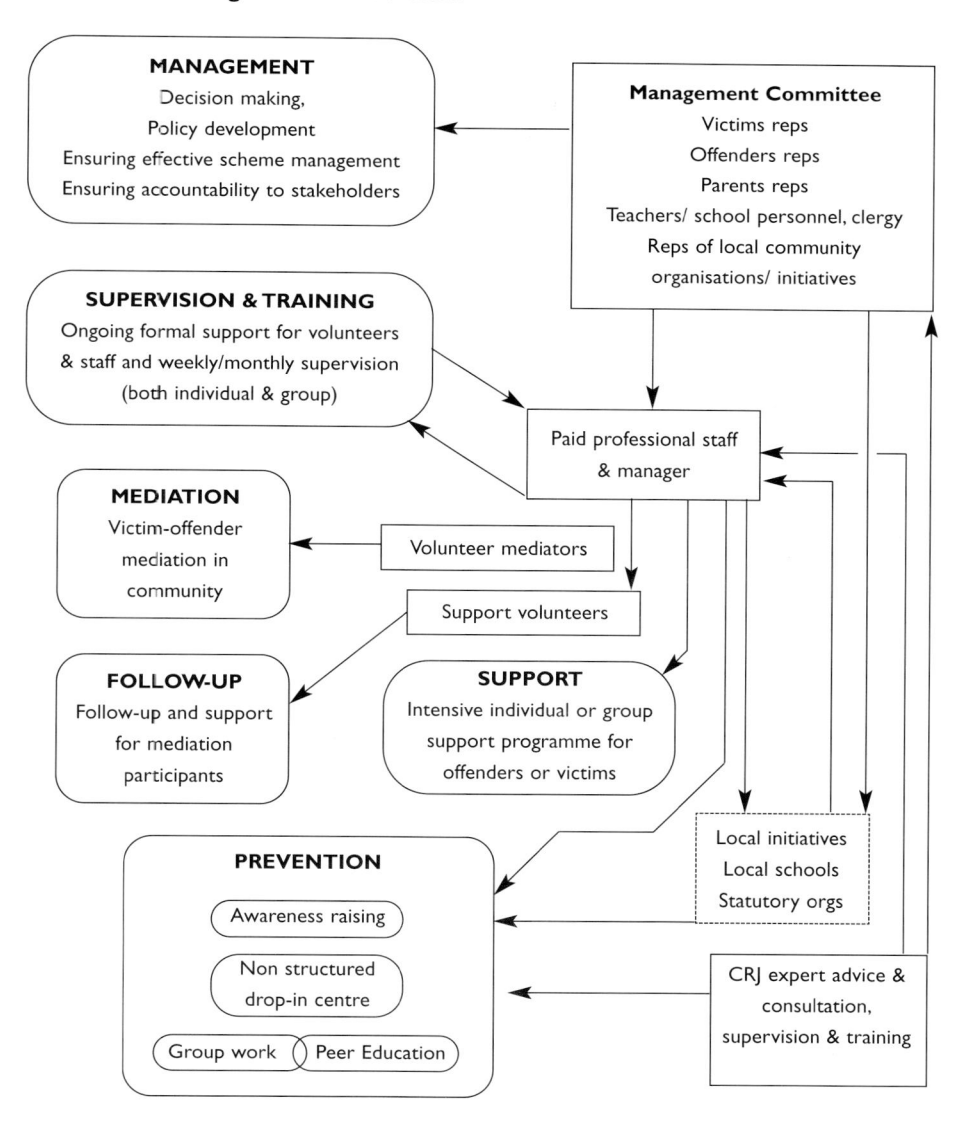

MANAGEMENT
Decision making,
Policy development
Ensuring effective scheme management
Ensuring accountability to stakeholders

Management Committee
Victims reps
Offenders reps
Parents reps
Teachers/ school personnel, clergy
Reps of local community
organisations/ initiatives

SUPERVISION & TRAINING
Ongoing formal support for volunteers
& staff and weekly/monthly supervision
(both individual & group)

Paid professional staff & manager

MEDIATION
Victim-offender
mediation in
community

Volunteer mediators

Support volunteers

FOLLOW-UP
Follow-up and support
for mediation
participants

SUPPORT
Intensive individual or group
support programme for
offenders or victims

Local initiatives
Local schools
Statutory orgs

PREVENTION
Awareness raising
Non structured drop-in centre
Group work   Peer Education

CRJ expert advice &
consultation,
supervision & training

Geography of CRJ Creggan

Figure 4.4 shows the 'geographical' layout of the proposed CRJ scheme in Creggan. The CRJ office is where staff and volunteers receive administrative and professional backup, and conduct meetings associated with the scheme. Separate but adjacent to this office it is proposed to locate a drop-in facility for young people, where an adult worker will be accessible to young people on an informal and ongoing basis. This facility would offer a space where young people could congregate and seek informal contact with one another and with the staff and volunteers. Clear parameters in terms of opening hours and limits of behaviour and its relationship with the CRJ office would have to be established for the operation of this facility. It is proposed that both the drop-in facility and the CRJ office will be located within Creggan, so that easy access and links with local homes, schools and schools can be established and maintained. The facilities must be accessible to local residents, community workers, teachers and to young people. The drop-in facility also must be distinct from the youth club, not only in its location, but also in terms of the 'looseness' of its structure. Often the young people involved in CRJ are unable to avail of traditional youth club facilities because of the structured nature of the programme. In a drop in facility, young people should have the freedom to engage in a range of activities or 'just talk' on an informal and spontaneous basis. Facilities for tea and coffee making, for listening to music, playing pool should be provided in the facility.

The CRJ scheme should also develop and maintain co-operative links with the statutory services including those parts of the justice system that are appropriate to work in the community. Formal referral and collaborative working relationships should be developed with all relevant agencies but especially with the Creggan Health Initiative Project (CHIP) and their health promotion programme for young people. Development of future joint work with such projects, which in turn could attract further funding, would be part of the responsibility of the paid CRJ workers.

The CRJ scheme by its very nature also needs to maintain close links with community leaders including those leaders who have the ear of local armed groups. This is an important aspect of being able to deliver non-violent intervention in the community. However, the delicate task of building a reputation of non-violent intervention, and developing a relationship of trust with the local community whereby the CRJ scheme has a track record of effective and non-violent work will take time to establish. Much suspicion, related to events in the past and associations of certain people in the community, must be overcome. It is important that trust develops, and yet it is also important that individuals in the community with a past association with violence are supported to create new and non-violent roles for themselves within the community. This is difficult but essential work, and lies at the core of peace-building. However, the work must be conducted with the greatest of sensitivity to the fears and reservations of local people, particularly young people. The facilitation of open and honest dialogue about these issues will undoubtedly form a part of the development of the scheme. Therefore, CRJ staff may be engaged in the facilitation of such dialogue and the promotion of such development in the community and schools.

Figure 4.4 GEOGRAPHY OF CRJ CREGGAN

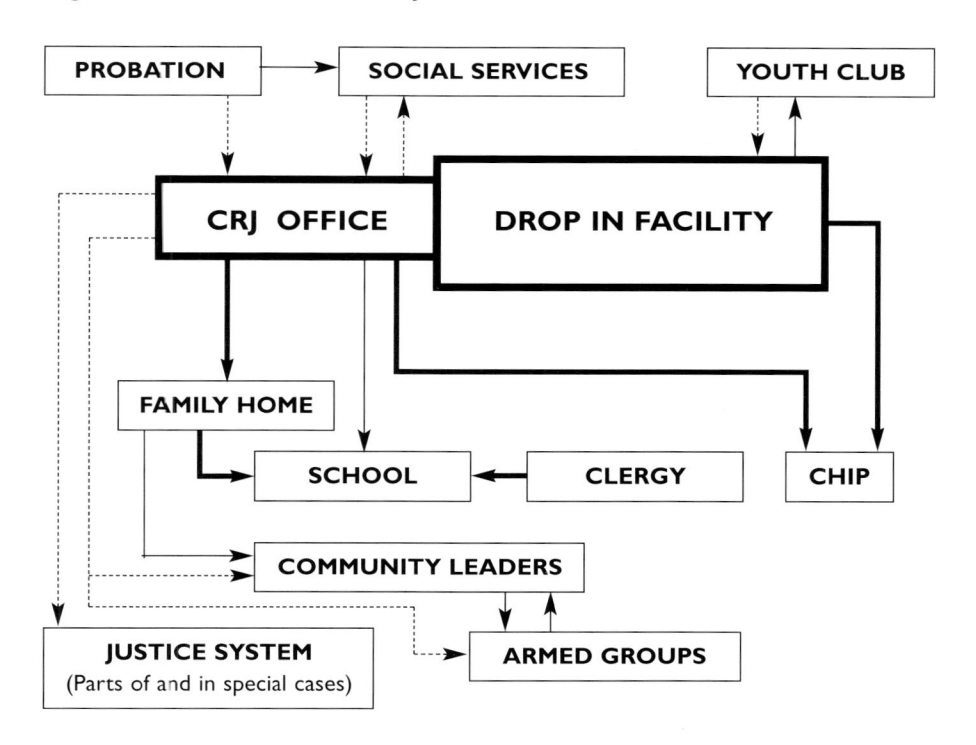

The Process of Building a Support Structure for the Work

All of the structures described above will require a range of task and processes to be set in motion. These are:

- Recruiting a representative group of volunteers to take the process forward;

- Consultation with local residents and representatives;

- Consultation with consumers of CRJ in Creggan;

- Consultation and eliciting support from other agencies and organisations active in the community and interested in the issues addressed by CRJ;

- Deliberation about the various views and reflection back to the stakeholders on emerging proposals for CRJ in Creggan;

- Finalising design and proposals for the scheme;

- Fund-raising;

- Training of committee, staff and volunteers;

- Recruitment of staff;

- Training of staff and volunteers;

- Securing of premises;

- Managing scheme on ongoing basis.

Principles

Out of our review of CRJ documentation, we would suggest that the following principles are particularly important in Creggan:

- Non-violent intervention;

- Healing relationships within the community and between the community and other agencies;

- Transparency and community accountability about the operation of the scheme (within the limits of confidentiality on individual cases or interventions);

- Confidentiality in relation to casework;

- A belief in the possibility of positive change in the lives of individuals and the community;

- Compassion, support and neighbourliness;

- Peace-building and dealing sensitively with the past;

- Support for all vulnerable community members;

- Collective responsibility for the quality of life in the community;

- Allowing people (and organisations) to change and do better or differently in the future than they have done in the past;

- Recognition and support for voluntary effort and for those who invest in the community's welfare;

- Identifying healthy and growth-promoting features of the community and supporting these;

- Identifying damaging aspects of community life, striving to understand the function they perform in the life of the community and finding and putting in place healthy replacements for them.

THE PROCESS OF BUILDING A SUPPORT STRUCTURE FOR THE WORK

Individual meetings with interested parties:- local teachers, clergy, business people, parents, victims and offenders: & ask them to audit local resources

First meeting of interested individuals & compilation of findings of resources audit: & visioning of aims of CRJ Creggan

Out of that group, appointment and induction of a local management committee composed of:
- ∞ Representatives of local schools/ teachers/principals
- ∞ Local Initiative representative
- ∞ Parents representative
- ∞ Young person's representative
- ∞ Offender's representative
- ∞ Victims' representative
- ∞ Independent chairperson whose role would be to facilitate participation of other members

Induction includes trips to see CRJ schemes in operation in other areas (suggest team of 8-12) and where appropriate links with other organisations *

Visit to Creggan of training team with CRJ expertise: Provision of in-house workshops for local management committee plus a one/two day conference in Creggan for all interested parties including local residents*

Production of vision statement for Creggan CRJ and draft proposal for community & interagency consultation. *

↓

Dissemination of vision statement and draft proposal in Creggan and beyond. Consultation process in three parts, namely:
1. a consultation, in which views are specifically
    - sought from: e.g
    - partnership boards
    - statutory agencies
    - individual victims
    - other service providers in statutory and voluntary sector
    - juvenile justice system
    - other relevant interests
2. A series of public meetings in Creggan in the City Centre, where the vision statement and proposal are presented and views canvassed and recorded
3. Consultation with experienced independent international expert(s) e.g. Harry Mika who may facilitate and consult with the group on a regular basis in the course of their work.
4. A call for members for the management committee
    - an invitation to organisations and to individuals who wish to work on the management committee in Creggan in taking forward the initiative and in managing it.

THE CONSULTATION PROCESS should be cumulative (snowballing), so that consulters evolve a cognate view and check it against the views of subsequent consultees. *

↓

Establishment, of committee: induction of members, team building, visioning and legal establishment of management committee

↓

Production and costing of final proposal *
Fund-raising begins

---

* ICR can facilitate / organise these processes/events

References

Auld, J., Gormally, B., McEvoy, K., and Ritchie, M. (1997) <u>Designing a System of Restorative Community Justice in Northern Ireland,</u> Belfast: NIACRO.

<u>Meeting Local Needs - A report into poverty and deprivation in the Creggan Area, Derry.</u> Creggan Neighbourhood Partnership (1996).

Kizilos, P (1998) <u>Nation in Transition: World in Conflict.</u> Johannesburg: Lerner.

Knox, C. and Quirk, P. (2000) <u>Peacebuilding in Northern Ireland, Israel and South Africa: Transition, Transformation and Reconciliation.</u> London: Palgrave.

Michie, J. (1997) <u>The Political Economy of South Africa's Transition</u>. Dryden.

Moholo, B. (2000<u>) Urban NGOs in Transition: The Case of South Africa</u>. INTRAC.

Thornton, C. 'Let the Battle Commence for the undecided voters.' *Belfast Telegraph*, Tuesday May 22, 2001 Page 6

Wall, D. (1999) 'A Story of the Navajo Justice System', in NIACRO <u>Reflections on Restorative Justice in the Community.</u> Belfast: NIACRO.

Appendix 1: Community Restorative Justice Questionnaire

For Researcher's Information:

Gender: Male ☐   Female ☐

Age: under 12yrs ☐   12 - 14yrs ☐   15 - 17yrs ☐   18 - 20yrs ☐
      21 - 25yrs ☐   25 - 30yrs ☐   31 - 35yrs ☐   36 - 39yrs ☐
      40 - 50yrs ☐   50yrs+ ☐

CRJ Scheme: Victim ☐   Offender ☐   Mediator ☐   Other ☐

Questions:

1. **Do you know what Community Restorative Justice is?**
   ☐ Yes   ☐ No

2. **Do you think it is a good alternative to a police force?**
   ☐ Yes   ☐ No

3. **Do you think that it is a non-violent approach to deal with problems in the community?**
   ☐ Yes   ☐ No

4. Do you think that it works well?
   ☐ Yes   ☐ No

5. Do you think that **CRJ** has any effect on crime levels?
   ☐ Yes   ☐ No

6. Do you think that it works for serious crimes?
   ☐ Yes   ☐ No

7. **Do you think that it works for minor crimes?**

   ☐ Yes   ☐ No

8. **Do you think that it works for all crimes?**

   ☐ Yes   ☐ No

9. **Do you think that it doesn't work for any crimes?**

   ☐ Yes   ☐ No

10. **Do you think that CRJ is a good idea?**

    ☐ Yes   ☐ No

11. **Do you agree with how CRJ is run in the Creggan?**

    ☐ Yes   ☐ No

12. **Do you think that the CRJ workers are good at sorting out problems in a non-violent way?**

    ☐ Yes   ☐ No

13. **Would you like the local CRJ scheme to be improved?**

    ☐ Yes   ☐ No

14. **Do you think the CRJ scheme needs to get more money so that it can be run better?**

    ☐ Yes   ☐ No

15. **Would you like to see other people running the scheme?**

    ☐ Yes   ☐ No

16. Are you satisfied with the way complaints are dealt with?

    ☐ Yes   ☐ No

17. Does the scheme always find out who really 'dunnit'?

    ☐ Yes   ☐ No

18. Do you think that the offenders are dealt with fairly?

    ☐ Yes   ☐ No

19. Do you think that **CRJ** is better than punishment beatings?

    ☐ Yes   ☐ No

20. Does **CRJ** reduce anti-social behaviour?

    ☐ Yes   ☐ No

21. Have you any direct experience of the **CRJ** scheme?

    ☐ Yes   ☐ No

22. If yes, did your experience change your views of the **CRJ**?

    ☐ Yes   ☐ No

Thank you for answering the questions

Appendix 2: Questionnaire: Creggan Report

1. **What is Community Restorative Justice?**
   a. a non-violent way of dealing with law and order problems in the community? ☐
   b. a way of getting people to pay for their crimes? ☐
   c. a good alternative to the RUC ☐
   d. a good alternative to punishment beatings? ☐
   e. don't know ☐

2. **How well does Community Restorative Justice work?**
   a. it works OK with minor crimes but is no use for violence or things like rape ☐
   b. it works for the offender but not for the victim ☐
   c. it has no real effect on crime levels in the community ☐
   d. don't know ☐

3. **Do you think that CRJ is a good idea? Do you agree with it?**
   a. it is a good idea until we get a proper police force ☐
   b. those who run it have no right to set themselves up the way they do ☐
   c. it is much better in the long run to any other form of policing. We should make it the permanent way to deal with local crime ☐
   d. it is a good idea that local people run schemes to deal locally with local problems ☐
   e. it would be OK or better if the police were involved in it ☐
   f. it might work in some other communities or countries but it is no use in Creggan ☐
   g. other (please explain) ☐

4. **Are there problems with CRJ?**
    a. no problems ☐
    b. it is not a deterrent to crime ☐
    c. it does not satisfy victims of crime ☐
    d. it rewards wrongdoing ☐
    e. it is run by the wrong people ☐
    f. it is in competition with the legitimate police force ☐
    g. it can't deal with serious crime ☐
    h. other (please explain) ☐

5. **How would you improve the local CRJ scheme?**
    a. make the penalties tougher ☐
    b. make the penalties lighter ☐
    c. make it more well known ☐
    d. give more money to those who run it ☐
    e. let victims run it ☐
    f. other (please explain) ☐

6. **How does CRJ compare to punishment beatings?**
    a. it is more acceptable because it is non-violent ☐
    b. it doesn't work as well as a deterrent, because the only thing some of these kids understand is a good beating ☐
    c. it doesn't set up a battle of wills between young people and paramilitaries ☐
    d. it keeps paramilitaries out of the picture and this is good ☐
    e. it keeps paramilitaries out of the picture and this is bad ☐
    f. it is the way forward in a society building peace ☐

7. Would you rather stick with punishment beatings?
    a. no, they are too brutal ☐
    b. no, they are bad publicity for the republican movement ☐
    c. no, because violence leads to more violence ☐
    d. yes, they work better in the long run as a method of tackling crime ☐
    e. yes, it keeps the paramilitaries in a central role ☐
    f. other (please explain) ☐

8. How does/would being involved in a CRJ scheme make you feel?
    a. like a 'bad' person ☐
    b. as if I had a way out of my difficulties ☐
    c. as if I had a chance to understand why someone did what they did to me ☐
    d. it would lessen my fears about being a victim ☐
    e. it would lessen my fears about being punished ☐
    f. it would help to make sense of my past difficulties ☐
    g. it would give me status in the community ☐
    h. other (please explain) ☐

9. What do you/ might you get out of being involved in a CRJ scheme?
    a. make new friends ☐
    b. understand other peoples' point of view ☐
    c. develop a positive relationship with adults ☐
    d. have somewhere to go and something to do ☐
    e. might help to put things to rights after what happened to me ☐
    f. other (please explain) ☐